Becoming a Conflict Competent Leader

Craig E. Runde

Tim A. Flanagan

JB JOSSEY-BASS

Center for
Creative
Leadership

NORTH AMERICA EUROPE ASIA
www.ccl.org

Becoming a Conflict Competent Leader

How You and Your Organization Can Manage Conflict Effectively

BICENTENNIAL
1807
WILEY
2007
BICENTENNIAL

John Wiley & Sons, Inc.

Published by Jossey-Bass
A Wiley Imprint
989 Market Street, San Francisco, CA 94103-1741   www.josseybass.com

Jossey-Bass books and products are available through most bookstores. To contact Jossey-Bass directly call our Customer Care Department within the U.S. at 800-956-7739, outside the U.S. at 317-572-3986, or fax 317-572-4002.

Jossey-Bass also publishes its books in a variety of electronic formats. Some content that appears in print may not be available in electronic books.

Library of Congress Cataloging-in-Publication Data
Runde, Craig E., 1951-
  Becoming a conflict competent leader : how you and your organization can manage conflict effectively / By Craig E. Runde and Tim A. Flanagan.
     p. cm.
  "A Joint Publication of The Jossey-Bass Business & Management Series and The Center for Creative Leadership."
  Includes bibliographical references and index.
  ISBN-13: 978-0-7879-8470-0 (cloth)
  ISBN-10: 0-7879-8470-1 (cloth)
  1. Leadership—Psychological aspects—Study and teaching. 2. Conflict management—Study and teaching. 3. Interpersonal conflict—Study and teaching. I. Flanagan, Tim A., 1955- II. Title.
HD57.7.R86 2007
658.4'092—dc22

                                                    2006020991

Printed in the United States of America
FIRST EDITION
HB Printing   10 9 8 7 6 5 4 3 2 1

A Joint Publication of

The Jossey-Bass

Business & Management Series

and

The Center for Creative Leadership

To Kathy, Matthew, Mac, Lindsay, and Kyle

Contents

Foreword

Since the Center for Creative Leadership launched its publishing alliance with Jossey-Bass in 1997, we have published a series of books—seventeen at last count—drawing on the research and educational work of CCL's large faculty. This work has greatly benefited from the contributions of our colleagues working independently or at other organizations. We have always hoped, once we had securely established the series, to expand it to include their work. With the present book, this hope is realized.

Let me give you a little background on the relationship between this book and CCL.

In the year 2000, the CCL open enrollment program Foundations of Leadership (FOL) was being revised. This program develops individuals who are new to leadership positions, and it had always addressed conflict management. From surveys of past participants and by examining assessment results and market research, we saw that conflict was the number one topic for new leaders. Most were in positions where they had little authority and great responsibility. They were asking us to help them with skills to better handle conflict so that they could be successful in their new leadership roles.

Because our programs emphasize assessment for development, the FOL team began a search for an instrument that would assess conflict-management skills. We knew of some that would assess conflict style. What we needed was one that looked at specific behaviors involving conflict so that leaders could receive feedback on their level of skill and then set a course of action to improve their performance. We found one from Eckerd College in St. Petersburg, Florida, that was in the finishing stages: the Conflict Dynamics Profile (CDP). (Eckerd College is a longtime CCL Network Associate authorized to offer the FOL program.)

The CDP provided a model and feedback on behaviors that are constructive in defusing and resolving conflict. It also looked at how leaders react to conflict over time, including hot buttons that can spark conflict, and the impact of certain behaviors within a leader's own organizational context. Added to the data were verbatim comments regarding individual strengths and development areas for managing conflict.

Implemented into the FOL program in 2001, the CDP has helped catalyze increased learning for our participants and enhanced their overall effectiveness as leaders. Participants explore specific actions for becoming more constructive in their approaches to conflict and learn how to minimize those actions that escalate conflict or, in some cases, derail their careers.

In this book, Craig E. Runde and Tim A. Flanagan define conflict as "any situation in which people have incompatible interests, goals, principles, or feelings." If you couple that with today's desire for more collaborative approaches to leadership, it is inevitable that conflicts will arise. How we handle them has widespread implications for individual leaders and the organizations they serve. Runde and Flanagan's book is a great starting place for the self-assessment and reflection needed to begin to improve one's skill level in dealing with conflict. Its message is timely and highly relevant for all who assume positions of leadership.

August 2006

John R. Alexander
President
Center for Creative Leadership

Preface

As part of our work at the Leadership Development Institute at Eckerd College (LDI), a network associate of the renowned Center for Creative Leadership (CCL), we work with highly successful managers and executives from major companies, government agencies, and nonprofit organizations. During our programs, we encourage participants to explore their strengths as well as possible areas for improvement. This focus on self-awareness is supported by assessment instruments that seek feedback from colleagues at work and fellow program participants.

Over the years, it has never ceased to amaze us how many of our participants have special difficulty with one particular element of leadership: dealing effectively with conflict. Some try to avoid it and wish it would just go away. Others tend to get angry and lash out at others in ways they later regret. These methods for dealing with conflict should not be surprising since conflict is a difficult area for most people. Our colleagues at CCL have noticed similar patterns. As a result of our experiences, LDI sponsored the development of a new conflict assessment instrument and created new programs on leadership and conflict management.

As we interacted with others in the training and development and conflict management fields, one thing became apparent: a large need for improving the conflict management skills of people in organizations. The costs of poorly managed conflict are high in financial terms. The costs are equally as high in terms of the quality of working relationships and morale. Although there are already many books and programs that do a good job of helping people improve the way they deal with conflict, many still just do not seem to handle conflict well. We also heard laments from trainers about the difficulty of getting buy-in from decision makers for such programs.

We came to believe what was needed was a call to action for leaders. Rather than waiting for training and development staff to sell the leader on the need for such a program, we came to believe that effective leaders should spearhead the effort by asking how soon they could get this kind of training in their organization. As we explored the issue, it became clear that leaders would need to do more than just ask questions. They would need to become more proficient in the ways they personally handle conflict, and they would need to understand the basics about how to ensure that their organization becomes conflict competent.

These observations led us to write this book. It should be noted that we always considered this a leadership book that deals with conflict management—rather than a text on conflict management. There are already a number of excellent books on conflict management, many of which we cite in this book. So if you want to become an expert on conflict management, we recommend reading them. Our intention here is different: we want leaders to recognize the importance of becoming conflict competent as a means to becoming a better leader. We want to provide them with a basic understanding of what is involved in becoming conflict competent from a personal as well as an organizational standpoint. Finally, we want them to champion change to help their organization improve the way in which conflict is handled so they can experience the many benefits that flow from conflict competence.

Personal Responses to Conflict

Conflict. What do you think or feel when you hear the word? If you are like most other people, you will probably experience some discomfort. The fact is that conflict can involve uncomfortable emotions and threaten relationships.

Leaders are no different. Our organization has trained thousands of leaders over the years, and time and again, they have told us that their most difficult workplace issue is conflict management. Yet as we will see, leaders are the key to improving their organizations' ability to deal effectively with conflict.

Does your organization handle conflict as well as you would like? Most do not. Poorly managed conflict creates enormous costs in the form of wasted management time, higher turnover, lawsuits, and the like. It can also lower productivity. When people are engaged in destructive conflict, they begin to pull back, stop sharing information, and take fewer risks. The result can be poorer-quality decision making. Lowered morale and strained working relationships can cause stress and sap employees' energy to focus on being creative and productive.

We do not think it is possible to do away with conflict. People will always have differences in values, goals, principles, and tactics that lead to conflict. The key becomes how they deal with these differences. Our experience suggests that when emotions get the best of people, they often use fight-or-flight types of responses that enflame and prolong conflict. For many people, their first instinct causes them to behave in counterproductive ways. It is as though many of our gut-level responses to conflict no longer serve us well in organizational settings. There are other approaches.

Libraries are full of excellent books on how to control emotions and engage in conflict constructively. If we read and actually acted on their advice, businesses (and the rest of the world) would be much better places. In many ways, effective conflict management is very simple. The types of techniques and behaviors that change conflict from a blaming contest to a collaborative problem-solving exercise are straightforward. In some ways, they seem self-evident, but for the most part, people do not embrace them naturally. As a consequence, organizations continue to suffer the many ills that stem from poorly managed conflict.

We suggest that left alone, the situation will not change. If you try to avoid conflict, it will not go away; it will just fester. If you do not systematically address the way in which your organization deals with conflict, it will continue to endure the ongoing costs of conflict or even experience a crisis (a strike, lawsuit, or media debacle, for example) precipitated by the buildup of unresolved conflict.

We believe that in order for this to change, leaders must engage in improving their own conflict awareness and skills as well as those of their organization. In other words, they need to become conflict competent leaders. They cannot afford to wait for others to raise the issue. Instead, they must show the way.

This book demonstrates the importance of developing conflict competence as a leadership skill. We share research results that found a strong correlation between effective leadership and constructive engagement in conflict. We want leaders, as well as those who provide leadership and conflict management training, to appreciate the importance of conflict competence.

Most of this book looks at how and what leaders need to do to become personally competent in dealing with conflict. Personal transformation is a crucial first step; without it, their efforts to champion conflict competence in their organization will ring hollow.

Chapter One looks at what conflict competent leadership is all about and why it is of such critical importance to organizations. Chapter Two introduces the basic dynamics of conflict and provides grounding in the subject. It is not enough to just understand conflict concepts, though. Self-awareness and self-control are key first steps in the transformational process. These subjects are the focus of Chapter Three.

Chapters Four and Five are the heart of the skill development portion of the book. They explore the behavioral skills that can make or break effective conflict management. Chapter Four looks at how leaders can lessen destructive responses, and Chapter Five shows how to use more constructive behaviors.

In Chapter Six we introduce ways in which leaders can help build conflict competence in their organizations. We examine methods for systematically improving the manner in which organizations manage conflict, as well as specific steps conflict competent leaders can take to encourage and foster positive change.

Above all, this book is meant to be a call to action to leaders. It provides a rationale and a basic road map for creating conflict competent leaders. Reading this book alone will just be a start. We have included a list of resources at the end of the book that will enable you to take the practical steps needed to develop your conflict management skills. You do not have to become an expert in all facets of conflict. By personally working to improve your skills and encouraging organizationwide initiatives, you can begin to improve the overall conflict competence of your organization and reap the benefits that effective conflict management brings.

Acknowledgments

We take this opportunity to acknowledge the many people who helped make this book possible. First, we thank our family members—Virginia "Mac," Lindsay, and Kyle Flanagan, and Kathy and Matthew Runde—for putting up with us or making do without us during the long periods of writing and editing. We are also grateful to Mac and Kathy for their help in proofreading the original manuscript.

We are indebted to Sal Capobianco, Mark Davis, and Linda Kraus, who developed the Dynamic Conflict Model and Conflict Dynamics Profile assessment instrument, a cornerstone for our approach to conflict management. Their ideas and encouragement inspired us to undertake and persevere in this effort. We express our appreciation to our friends and colleagues Dan Dana, Jennifer Lynch, and Cinnie Noble. These conflict management experts opened our eyes to new approaches to dealing more effectively with conflict and allowed us to use their ideas in writing this book.

We thank our colleagues at the Leadership Development Institute who supported our efforts: James Deegan, Margaret Cooley, Jennifer Hall, Megan Watson Kramer, Nancy Pridgen, Sheila McLaughlin, Andi Kuhn, Ashley Calvert Yeager, Kuuipo Salisbury-Hammon,

Arlene Miller, Regina Pheil, Jackie Parham, Patty Viscomi, Bev Smith, Kristin Williams, Jenny Dunbeck, and Becky Alderman.

Finally, we thank Sara King and Martin Wilcox from the Center for Creative Leadership who introduced us to Kathe Sweeney, our wonderful editor at Jossey-Bass. Kathe, Jessie Mandle, and Mary Garrett from Jossey-Bass helped us throughout the process and made writing the book much easier than we had imagined.

St. Petersburg, Florida   Craig E. Runde
August 2006   Tim A. Flanagan

Becoming a Conflict
Competent Leader

1

THE WHAT AND WHY OF CONFLICT COMPETENT LEADERS

Difficulties are meant to rouse, not discourage. The human spirit is to grow strong by conflict.

—*William Ellery Channing*

The basic nature of human beings is to avoid painful or unpleasant experiences whenever possible. How many different versions of, "I'd rather go to the dentist than [fill in the blank]," have you heard in your life? For most of us, dealing with conflict ranks right up there with impromptu public speaking or firing an employee. If you've ever filled in the blank above with anything resembling "deal with conflict," you're in exceptionally good company.

So what might motivate a leader to strive toward conflict competence? First, we believe that conflict in the workplace is bound to occur, so you may as well equip yourself with the skills to deal with it. Your workplace may be a Fortune 500 company or a family-owned small business. It may be government offices, schools, or nonprofit agencies. It really doesn't matter because conflict occurs in all workplaces. In our work at the Eckerd College Leadership Development Institute (LDI), we have had the opportunity to interact with thousands of executives, directors, managers, and team leaders engaged in their personal leadership development processes. What we have learned from them about leadership and conflict, stated simply, is this: conflict is inevitable for leaders, and it exists at the root of some of their best ideas and at the core of many of their worst failures.

Second, the effects of conflict are dramatic on both human resources and the bottom line. So there is a level of leadership responsibility involved in addressing conflict. Effective leaders hold themselves accountable for establishing work environments that provide safety and respect while helping the organization meet business and financial goals. Handling conflict effectively encompasses both of these objectives.

Third, despite the avoidance response most of us experience when engaging in conflict, not all conflict is negative, painful, or unpleasant. On the contrary, harnessing the power of conflict can be the catalyst for new ideas and creative solutions to challenging business issues. Jeff Weiss and Jonathon Hughes (2005) suggest that "executives underestimate not only the inevitability of conflict but also—and this is key—its importance to the organization. The disagreements sparked by differences in perspective, competencies, access to information, and strategic focus within a company actually generate much of the value that can come from collaboration across organizational boundaries. Clashes between parties are the crucibles in which creative solutions are developed and wise trade-offs among competing objectives are made" (p. 2). In other words, wise leaders should embrace conflict and find ways to encourage the proliferation of differences as a strategy that enables the organization to get and stay ahead.

Both the science and art of leadership have been studied and chronicled for decades. There are a myriad of models, definitions, theories, and concepts regarding leadership. Who among us doesn't recall the great discussions focused on leadership versus management? Is a leader a manager? Is a manager a leader? Do leaders manage? Can managers lead? Today most of us agree that there are key differences in how we view leadership and management. Nevertheless, the study of leadership and management shows no signs of slowing. In fact, over thirty-five hundred new management books are published each year (Pfeffer, 2005). In order to describe the conflict competent leader effectively, it seems appropriate to begin with a brief discussion of leadership.

Because we work in the field of leadership development, we prefer to think in terms of experiences, growth, and learning rather than a linear definition of leadership. It makes sense, though, to identify our broad definition of leaders. We believe leaders are those whose roles in organizations include accountability for influencing others or establishing structure for others to follow, or those who are recognized for developing priorities for the organization. In most cases, leaders have formal role designations or titles: team leader, supervisor, manager, director, vice president, or president. In short, we believe leaders are best identified by those who look to them for leadership. If you are a person who is consistently looked to for leadership, you are most likely a leader.

Leaders constantly learn from their experiences and actively seek opportunities for development. Leadership development has been defined at the Center for Creative Leadership as the "expansion of a person's capacity to be effective in leadership roles and processes" (McCauley, Moxley, and Van Velsor, 1998, p. 25). The expansion of these capabilities occurs over time and is usually maximized through a variety of experiences that provide challenge, support, and opportunities to learn. And certainly context is important in shaping the development process. The most successful leaders continue to learn throughout their careers. They become aware of their most effective strengths and use them relentlessly. They are just as aware of their limitations, or "developmental opportunities," and strive to improve, or in some cases minimize, the effects of these limitations.

For many leaders, the area of conflict presents one of their most demanding challenges. This makes sense considering the sheer volume of conflict opportunities that leaders face. Leaders can find themselves in personal conflicts with others in the organization. They are also sought out to mediate conflicts among their direct reports or peers. Leaders are often asked for advice about how to handle conflicts or are looked to for conflict coaching. At times, they must grapple with conflict involving vendors, clients, or other stakeholders. At other times, they must consider the culture in their organizations, which may include assessing how conflict is treated at a strategic or systems level. Furthermore, the costs and opportunities associated with conflict demand the attention of leaders. Because conflict is so often emotionally charged, there is a sense of urgency when it occurs, so it attracts leadership attention immediately. And conflict is frequently not resolved quickly, so leaders find themselves involved for substantial periods of time. Conflict definitely qualifies as a demanding leadership challenge.

The relationship between leadership and conflict appears natural and inevitable. It is our belief that defining conflict in broad terms makes the most sense for discussing its relationship to leadership. With this in mind, we refer to the work of our colleagues Sal Capobianco, Mark Davis, and Linda Kraus, the creators of the Conflict Dynamics Profile. The Conflict Dynamics Profile is a groundbreaking 360-degree assessment instrument that provides feedback on individuals' behaviors before, during, and after conflict. Its creators define conflict as, "any situation in which people have incompatible interests, goals, principles or feelings" (Capobianco, Davis, and Kraus, 1999, p. 1). This definition certainly encompasses many different situations and contexts, as do a leader's role and scope. Leaders confront conflicts that arise regarding both short-term and long-standing issues, handle disagreements about strategies and tactics, and referee struggles for resources. They also discover conflict resulting from misperceptions, misinterpretations, misunderstandings, and miscommunications among people. It appears that conflicts can result from almost anything that puts at least two people in opposition.

In addition to handling conflicts among others, leaders often find themselves in disagreement with somebody about something. This is not to disparage those wonderful moments when everybody is "on board," the team is "flying in tight formation," or the entire organization is "marching in the same direction." These are times to savor and reinforce. Realistically, though, the notion of 100 percent buy-in is a lofty goal. When complete buy-in or agreement isn't possible, why not respond as one of our close associates does

with a hearty, "That's great! We see it differently!" As we have suggested above, conflicts and disagreements present opportunities and
should not be avoided. Some kinds of conflict can be productive
and are at the very heart of creative ideas, innovative approaches, and
previously unseen possibilities. Differing opinions and diverse perspectives can lead to new solutions and unexpected breakthroughs.
Or conflict can become destructive when the disagreeing parties
don't handle their differences effectively. This dichotomy is at the
fulcrum of the leader's most crucial challenges when developing
conflict competence. How do leaders encourage the exploration of
differing viewpoints while minimizing the hazards of polarization?
How do they know when to intervene in a dispute between or
among others? What are the signs that a conflict is getting out of
control? How do leaders stay attuned to their personal reactions and
behaviors when they are involved in a conflict? Are there ways to
construct effective organizational approaches to conflict? We believe
that conflict competent leaders understand the dynamics of conflict,
are aware of their strengths and developmental opportunities for
handling personal conflict, model appropriate behaviors when engaged in conflict, find ways to foster constructive responses among
others while reducing or avoiding destructive responses, and encourage the development of a conflict competent organization through
systems and culture.

How does a leader acquire the skills and experience to develop
this area of competency? Acquiring experience, if you agree with
the notion that conflict is inevitable, will not be a problem. Lead
long enough (we suspect a few days at most will be enough), and
you will encounter conflict. A participant in one of our conflict
workshops commented in the program evaluation, "I won't have to
look very hard to find opportunities to practice the approaches I've
learned in this class." Acquiring experience is not the issue.

Acquiring the skills is the primary challenge. And leaders who
are conflict competent don't just "acquire" skills. They study, hone,
and develop their skills over time as they encounter experience after
experience. True to our leadership development roots, we believe

the most effective practices for developing competence are centered on exposure to a variety of developmental experiences coupled with the ability to learn. In one of the most extensive and revered studies of executive development, *The Lessons of Experience* (1988), McCall, Lombardo, and Morrison categorized the key developmental experiences of leaders into three sets of lessons: assignments, the impact of others, and hardships.

Anyone using this framework can begin to imagine the variety of conflict experiences associated with each category. The assignments people accept during a career can be rife with conflict. How often are aspiring leaders given the challenge to "fix" an existing problem? Or "take over" a floundering project? Or present to an unfriendly audience? Or accept a new role with little or no training? A leader in any one of these cases can be instantly engulfed by the conflicting viewpoints of resistant workers, unhappy customers, or feuding colleagues. During a recent workshop, the general manager of a restaurant described the conflicting priorities she faced while opening a new facility: "I needed to keep the pressure on my assistant managers to complete the hiring of new employees by the deadline while at the same time insisting that they manage the training of existing employees in order to open the restaurant on time. I'm sure they thought I was unfair, unfeeling, and uncompromising in my approach. But what choice did I have? We had to have a critical mass hired and we had to have the staff trained. There was no way I was going to be unprepared to open on time. As it turned out, we had a great opening, but I worry that I damaged some relationships along the way."

When considering the impact of others, most leaders are able to quickly identify people who provided positive models of accomplishment as well as those who were negative models. In later chapters, we explore the impact of constructive and destructive behaviors on conflict situations. For most of us, it is easy to recall the actions of others that demonstrate both sets of behavior.

Finally, lessons learned as a result of hardships can be associated readily with conflict situations. Most leaders are able to identify events or periods of time they describe as personal or career setbacks. A senior vice president at a major high-tech firm with whom we worked described his greatest challenge over the final few months of his tenure like this: "I'd estimate that 70 percent of my work-related energy was spent on managing the lousy relationship I had with my boss. We just didn't seem to see anything eye-to-eye. Not only did I constantly battle him at work, but I found that I'd carry the negativity home with me every day, and it began to spill over with my family and friends. I didn't know it at the time, but my wife later told me I was like a flea carrying the plague. Every person I touched was likely to be infected by the conflict I was bringing home from work." Although not all setbacks and hardships are the direct result of conflict, it is reasonable to assert that they can provide the precipitating event or starting point for a conflict to develop.

We are certain that all leaders will experience conflict as they lead. In leadership development terms, those with an adequate ability to learn will be in positions to acquire, analyze, and apply knowledge to their experiences. This combination of experience and ability to learn are the ingredients that lead to skill development, which is necessary for becoming competent—in this case, conflict competent. Our purpose is not to review the extensive research and documentation about best leadership development practices. Rather, the bulk of this book explores what we have learned about conflict and how leaders develop the skills to become conflict competent.

Conflict Competency

We believe there are four distinct areas or skill sets that are required for a leader to be considered conflict competent:

- Understanding the dynamics of conflict
- Understanding his or her own reactions to conflict
- Fostering constructive responses to conflict (and reducing destructive responses)

- Creating a conflict competent organization

In the next few pages we provide an overview of these four areas. In Chapters Two through Six, we engage in a more detailed and thorough discussion of them. What follows is a brief overview of each skill set.

Understanding the Dynamics of Conflict

Conflict competent leaders do not have to be experts in the study of human behavior. They will benefit, though, from understanding the nature of some basic human responses such as "fight or flight" and the "retaliatory cycle." Many of us experience strong emotional reactions to conflict. At times our instinct is to dig in and defend our positions at all costs. When confronted with arguments different from our own, we respond by arguing equally or more vehemently for our side. This is the "fight" response. In other situations, we find our emotional barometer urging us to escape the conflict situation, avoiding the confrontation or disagreement as best we can. Removing ourselves from the conflict as completely as possible and avoiding the other party seems the only reasonable choice. This is the "flight" response.

There are times when despite our intentions (and the best intentions of our conflict partner), the conflict seems to spin more and more out of control into the ever-deepening chasm of irreconcilable differences. The nature of our communication and the perceptions of our conflict partner contribute insidiously to a pattern of responses that leads us down a path of negativity and destruction with little hope for resolution. This "retaliatory cycle" is observable, manageable, and reversible.

The key to applying this understanding of the dynamics of conflict lies in the ability to observe and detect a myriad of subtle human interaction cues. A raised eyebrow here or strain in the voice there may be the clues that alert the conflict competent leader to the potential conflict lurking just below the surface. The real trick is to monitor the clues and decide just how to respond. The conflict competent leader is adept at encouraging constructive conflict and equally skilled at handling conflict that becomes destructive.

Understanding One's Own Reactions to Conflict

It is especially crucial for conflict competent leaders to understand and embrace their own strengths and developmental opportunities in regard to conflict. The most effective leaders are known for being models of exemplary behavior. This notion has never been truer as it applies to conflict. Self-awareness is critical.

As human beings, we experience emotions. As individuals, we experience emotions in unique and profound ways. In addition, as human beings, we have the ability to reason. Each of us has our own "wiring" when it comes to thinking and reasoning. We are uniquely individual. In our individuality, we respond to conflict in cognitive and emotional ways. For leaders, it is of utmost importance to be aware of their personal reactions to conflict so they can manage their responses and model the most effective behaviors before, during, and after conflict. The way leaders are seen handling conflict sends strong signals to those around them about their ability to assist them when they experience conflict. In order to establish credibility as a conflict competent leader, it is imperative to model constructive engagement in conflict.

Fostering Constructive Responses to Conflict (and Reducing Destructive Responses)

One of the basic tenets of our work is this: people who are most effective at handling conflict behave in constructive ways. These constructive behaviors are identifiable, learnable, and applicable. The more you employ these constructive behaviors before, during, and after conflict, the more effective you become at handling conflict.

The work of Sal Capobianco, Mark Davis, and Linda Kraus (1999) presents two sets of behaviors associated with responses to conflict: constructive behaviors, which tend to reduce tension and keep the conflict focused on ideas and information rather than people, and destructive behaviors, which tend to make things worse and escalate the conflict. The focus shifts to personalities and people and away from ideas. As a metaphor, Capobianco, Davis, and Kraus suggest thinking of conflict as a fire: constructive behaviors help control the fire, and destructive behaviors fan the flames.

Capobianco, Davis, and Kraus have identified seven constructive behaviors and eight destructive behaviors. The constructive behaviors are perspective taking, creating solutions, expressing emotions, reaching out, reflective thinking, delay responding, and adapting. The destructive behaviors are winning at all costs, displaying anger, demeaning others, retaliating, avoiding, yielding, hiding emotions, and self-criticizing.

We will explore in depth how the use of constructive behaviors leads to favorable outcomes and the natural reduction of destructive behaviors. Conflict competent leaders will not only discover how to use constructive behaviors themselves, but will see the desirability of coaching others to do the same.

Creating a Conflict Competent Organization

The most effective leaders do more than model effective behaviors and influence or develop others. They also find ways to transform their organization's conflict culture. They champion the establishment of processes and systems that enable organizational conflict competence. In this case, conflict competent leaders support training, coaching, and mentoring at all levels. They espouse a systems approach to handling conflict and the use of a wide variety of approaches to resolving conflict.

We will explore the notion of organizational impact and reflect on the works of conflict management system design experts regarding the development of effective systems to address conflict. We believe that talented leaders make lasting, significant contributions to organizations. When they harness the tremendous upside of conflict while minimizing the potential for harm, the organization will reap benefits perhaps previously unimaginable.

Why Conflict Competent Leaders Are Needed

Organizations have long recognized that they need leaders with intelligence and technical proficiency. Recently, growing attention has been paid to the importance of the emotional aspects of leadership (Goleman, 1995). Our experience at LDI confirms this trend. Throughout the 1980s and 1990s, we surveyed executives and managers who attended our leadership development programs, asking about their toughest challenges. Time and again their responses focused on an issue that strikes at the heart of emotional intelligence: conflict management. They found conflict hard to handle because it is filled with difficult emotional issues that sometimes flare up and at others go underground.

Research involving LDI clients suggests that more effective leaders are better able than less effective leaders to address conflict. A study of more than three hundred managers found that the participants' bosses, peers, and direct reports rated them as more effective leaders when they were seen as exhibiting higher levels of constructive responses to conflict. Conversely, those who engaged in destructive types of responses were not seen as effective leaders. Similar connections have been drawn by other researchers based on field observations suggesting that those who have developed constructive approaches to conflict are viewed as leaders even when they do not hold formal leadership positions (Patterson, Grenny, McMillan, and Switzler, 2002).

We believe competency in dealing with organizational conflict is a hallmark of effective leaders and crucial to organizational success. The organizational costs associated with poorly handled conflict are too high to ignore.

The Costs of Conflict Incompetence

When conflict is mismanaged, costs mount. Some out-of-pocket costs like absenteeism and lawsuits are relatively easy to see and compute. Others, like poor decision making, lost opportunities, and diminished quality of working relationships, can prove more costly, though they are more difficult to quantify.

One obvious cost concerns management time wasted dealing with conflict rather than addressing more productive issues. Surveys by the CCL and LDI show that most managers estimate that between 20 and 40 percent of their time is spent dealing with conflict (Center for Creative Leadership, 2003; Runde, 2003), figures that are consistent with earlier management studies (Thomas and Schmidt, 1976; Watson and Hoffman, 1996). How and why does so much time get consumed?

One of our clients, whom we will call Mary, was frustrated because she was unable to focus on her main tasks. When asked what was diverting her attention, she complained that her subordinates were constantly coming to her to resolve conflicts. Mary was a good problem solver, so they approached her to fix their problems rather than resolving the issues by themselves. Although this worked well for the employees, it became a major drain on Mary's time and energy until she was finally able to use techniques described later in this book to lessen her burden. Her predicament illustrates one way that ineffective conflict management can waste managers' time.

A second conflict-related cost is the loss of employees. It has been estimated that more than half of employee retention problems are related to poorly handled conflict (Dana, 2005). When conflict creates morale problems and interferes with employees' abilities to do their jobs, they may look for a better place to work, particularly when the job market is strong. Many of these problems occur with the employee's manager. The replacement costs of finding, training, and bringing a new person up to speed can often exceed the annual salary of the employee who leaves. It certainly costs more than addressing conflicts in the first place so employees do not get frustrated and leave. If turnover becomes an organizational problem, an effective leader needs to determine if poorly managed conflict is at least partially at fault.

Absenteeism and health costs related to work stress also contribute to the financial toll caused by ineffectively managed conflict. One form of absenteeism represents an attempt to avoid dealing with conflict: the employee takes a sick day in order to delay or escape dealing with the unpleasant problem. Another aspect of absenteeism relates to actual physical or emotional distress or illness associated with conflict. Research has demonstrated a connection between workplace conflict and stress as well as the detrimental health effects of workplace stress (Quick, Quick, Nelson, and Hurrell, 1997; Yandrick, 1999). Health claims and their effects on insurance premiums as well as the productivity losses associated with absenteeism can constitute significant financial drains on organizations.

Grievances, complaints, and lawsuits often stem from ineffectively managed conflict. Many times the complainant just wants an opportunity to talk about the problem or receive an apology for a perceived wrong. If it is handled effectively at the start, the issue can be resolved informally with much less cost. Yet problems are often ignored or not handled well. Then the conflict spirals out of control and becomes a dispute that requires more formal third-party intervention, which can increase the time, effort, and cost required for resolution. Even if an organization prevails in such a dispute with an individual employee, vendor, or customer, it does not mean that the organization has won. The process, whether litigation or a less complicated approach such as mediation, can still take costly time for preparation and participation. In addition, there is always the possibility of losing on the merits, which can cost a great deal more.

Workplace conflict can lead to an even more extreme problem: workplace violence. The National Institute of Occupational Safety and Health (1997) estimates that more than one million workers are assaulted each year at work. A significant number of these assaults come from disgruntled customers, patients, coworkers, and employees. The emotional toll on the targets of the violence as well as to their coworkers can be enormous and can increase the costs associated with retention, absenteeism, and health care.

Many of these costs directly affect organizational productivity. When managers are spending their time dealing with conflict rather than developing new products or helping their employees serve customers, productivity lags. When workers brood at their desk about conflict issues, spend time complaining to coworkers about the conflict, stay home to avoid it, or even leave the organization when conflict becomes unbearable, the organization suffers too.

In one of our programs, we have participants estimate how much conflict currently costs their organization. We use the Dana Measure of Financial Cost of Organizational Conflict survey (Dana, 2006), which enables users to provide their own estimates for cost categories described in this chapter. Although they are encouraged to use conservative estimates for each of the cost categories, our participants are constantly surprised at the high cost of conflict their organizations incur. They say that their surprise comes in part because they had never systematically reviewed conflict-related expenses or at least had never consciously attributed them to poor conflict management.

Beyond Costs

While cost savings alone make a compelling case for leaders who can address conflict in an effective manner, there are additional reasons for leaders who are conflict competent. People operate differently in situations where conflict becomes destructive. These changes can disrupt the effective functioning of an organization. For example, when facing conflict, some people begin withholding information from those with whom they have conflict. When sharing begins to dry up, decisions may be made based on inadequate information. When the relationships become too tense, managers may feel compelled to reorganize work groups to separate individuals. This may temporarily relieve the tension, but it may be counterproductive to bringing the best talents to bear on the issues faced by a work group.

While most people think of conflict as negative, conflict theory suggests that there are creative opportunities that can emerge from conflict when it is managed effectively. Imagine what an organization would look like if it had absolutely no conflict at all—pretty boring and static. Some suggest that leaders need to make sure that there is sufficient debate and conflict in their organization to ensure that varying approaches to important issues are considered and appropriately vetted. The key in these cases is to stimulate debate without letting it become destructive or focused on personalities as opposed to the task at hand (Roberto, 2005). Conflict that involves the airing of different opinions can stimulate creativity as ideas feed off one another and new concepts emerge. When conflict can be used constructively to elicit ideas and appropriately challenge them, it can help prevent teams from falling into the trap of groupthink, where extreme concurrence seeking can lead to suppression of conflict and a consequent drop in the quality of decision making (Turner and Pratkanis, 1997). A classic example of this was the failure of the Swiss watchmaking industry to grasp the cutting-edge digital technology that became the new standard. The Swiss watchmakers decided that the new technology was a fad that wouldn't last. The Swiss experts needed little debate. They were convinced the technology was fallible because a watch without a mainspring certainly wouldn't work. Their decision resulted in a massive loss of market share from which the industry never fully recovered.

Effective strategic planning requires sharing information and debating the ideas developed from that information. Conflict avoidance causes both the information sharing and vetting to dry up and undermines the rigorous debate required for superior strategic decision-making quality (Amason and Schweiger, 1997). An organization sent a group of executives to LDI to work on examining their mission and vision. After several days, it became apparent to us that most of the executive team members refused to engage in any meaningful debate with the senior member of the team. They deferred to his opinions and yielded to his suggestions. We intervened by providing feedback about the lack of debate and suggested that the team examine how they handled conflict before proceeding with their primary objective. Eventually the team began sharing observations about their lack of open communication. They chose to table their examination of the mission and vision until after they had resolved their communication issues.

Effective conflict management can also be a key to stimulating a collaborative workplace environment. Disagreements inevitably arise when people from different parts of an organization begin working together. If these disagreements cannot be addressed in a successful manner, they will undermine collaboration and prevent the realization of benefits that conflict can bring (Weiss and Hughes, 2005). Conflict programming at LDI frequently focuses on engaging participants in exercises and simulations that elicit disagreements. We teach participants to employ approaches, techniques, and behaviors that enable successful resolution of differences. As participants find they can be successful in the classroom, they gain confidence that they can use the same approaches, techniques, and behaviors in the workplace.

When an organization is able to develop a culture that emphasizes the use of constructive conflict management and resolution internally, it also helps create an environment where employees will interact with customers, vendors, and other external parties in a more effective manner. If an organization espouses high customer service values but ignores or mismanages internal conflicts, employees are likely to look at these actions as their cues for how they are to deal with others. Once poor habits such as ignoring internal conflicts become ingrained, they can become a major obstacle to development of successful customer relations. But if an organization can align its internal conflict management strategies with the way it wants to treat it clients, then it can achieve higher-quality client interactions (J. Lynch, conversation with Craig Runde on Dec. 12, 2005).

Knowing how to engage and resolve conflict also helps build stronger relationships—with clients, with vendors, among employees, and between managers and employees. These relationships can help these interdependent parties become more creative and productive and can make work life more enjoyable. Strong relationships can better weather problems and allow people to look for ways for resolving conflicts that enable all parties to gain. The first step along this path is becoming familiar with the basic dynamics of conflict.

2

UNDERSTANDING CONFLICT DYNAMICS

Conflict is inevitable, but combat is optional.

—*Max Lucado*

Leaders do not need to become conflict experts, but it is important that they appreciate how and why people respond to conflict in the manner they do. This understanding will help illuminate the way to new, more effective kinds of responses that can turn conflict from a problem into an opportunity. In this chapter, we look at what conflict is, how people think about it, how it arises and unfolds, and how people respond to it. This basic grounding in conflict dynamics can help leaders better understand why they need to engage conflict rather than avoid it: to lessen its harmful effects while taking advantage of the opportunities inherent within conflict.

What Is Conflict?

In Chapter One, we introduced one definition of conflict: "any situation in which people have incompatible interests, goals, principles, or feelings" (Capobianco, Davis, and Kraus, 2001). Underpinning this and many other definitions of conflict is the notion of differences. These differences come in many forms. They include differences about fundamental values and principles. Often they focus on how to solve problems and get interests met. They may also involve differences in objectives, as well as tactics to meet them. Many differences come with a history laden with emotional baggage.

Think about a conflict that you've experienced recently. How would you describe the differences at play in it? While it is relatively easy to come up with reasons why the other person is wrong, it usually takes more effort to consider what lies behind the conflict in the first place. Taking time to think about the differences rather than focusing immediately on who is right or wrong can be beneficial.

The differences can come from a variety of sources. Sometimes they involve personal preferences people may have for the ways they like to do things or even the things they like to do. Some of these may be closely related to different personality traits. Have you ever been in conflict with others about how to solve a problem and wondered, "How in the world could they see things the way they do?" The other person may be thinking the same thing. In many cases, it may be that their preferred style of problem solving is different from yours. People can have legitimate differences in the way they approach things, and these differences can lead to conflict.

People can also have different values. These may lead to some of the most difficult conflicts since values make up an important part of our identity. Many of our major social conflicts (abortion, same-sex marriage, capital punishment) stem from value differences. These are so closely connected to our identities that they can easily arouse strong emotions. At times it seems impossible to concede because it would threaten our sense of identity.

Sometimes differences arise among people from various cultural or ethnic backgrounds. Sometimes when we engage with people from different backgrounds, it can be difficult to understand why they act as they do. Moreover, these differences can seem confusing and sometimes appear threatening. It is also easy to think that the perspectives of our own culture or background are right or appropriate to the solution of issues, whereas the others' approaches are not.

Incompatibility

It is not just differences that define conflict. Somehow the parties must perceive that the differences create a situation that will be contrary to their interests or needs. If the people do not currently care about the differences, there is still the potential for conflict. If you like the beach and your colleague prefers the mountains, it does not necessarily mean you will have conflict. It could, however, if you both have to jointly decide the location for your company's next retreat.

So the issue of incompatibility is added to the mix. If the needs of people differ and they are somehow incompatible—you getting your way means I will not get mine—then the situation is ripe for conflict. In fact, the situation requires only the appearance or perception of incompatibility for conflict to ensue. Have you ever experienced a conflict when you initially thought that the other person's interests and yours were incompatible, only to find out later that they were not? Our initial perceptions about situations can be affected by inadequate information, misunderstandings, or prejudices that can cause us to see incompatibility where there really is none. So it would be helpful to adjust the earlier definition of conflict to be "any situation in which people have *apparently* incompatible interests, goals, principles, or feelings."

The notion of incompatibility also implies the potential for the relationship to become competitive. When people have apparently incompatible goals, they often look at the situation as a zero-sum game. If the other person getting his or her way is seen as keeping you from getting your way, then let the competition begin! Indeed, some models look at competitive versus cooperative interaction as the key dichotomy in conflict (Deutsch and Coleman, 2000).

Interdependence

The aspect of incompatibility becomes more crucial in interdependent relationships. When situations involve someone with whom you have ongoing interactions, the stakes tend to be raised. You are no longer dealing with just the facts of the situation but also the ongoing relationship with the person.

Conflict, especially in organizational contexts, often arises between people who have interdependent relationships. If you have differences with someone you will never see again, they will likely be treated as a minor annoyance and quickly be forgotten. The same types of differences with someone with whom you work every day may lead to ongoing conflict. When we add this concept to our definition, we see conflict as "any situation in which *interdependent* people have apparently incompatible interests, goals, principles, or feelings."

How People Think About Conflict

While it is helpful to have a working definition of conflict, it is just as important to consider how people actually think about it. Although people often experience conflict and may mull over the specifics of a particular dispute, it is rarer that they reflect about conflict in the abstract.

We think it is important for leaders to begin to consider how they conceive of conflict, since this framework, expressed or not, will influence how they approach dealing with it. In our programs, we often ask participants to consider words that describe conflict for them. Take a moment to think about recent conflicts that you have experienced. Note some words that come to mind when you think conflict. Why do you think about these particular terms?

Our participants have come up with a large list of words to describe how they see conflict. In Exhibit 2.1 we present a list of the most common ones that they have used, as well as a few uncommon ones (Runde, 2005). Many of the words have some kind of negative connotation—for example, the ones dealing with anger, fear, frustration, and stress. Yet there are also terms in the list that suggest that there can be a silver lining to conflict: *opportunity, growth,* and *creativity.*

The vast majority of our participants list primarily negative words to describe conflict. Were some of your words of this type? Why might so many more people think first of these negative elements? This may stem from the emotions that people feel when faced with conflict. A sense of potential differences can often lead us to get angry toward another person or to become afraid of confrontation. Or we might not want to acknowledge the existence of

Exhibit 2.1 Words Used to Describe Conflict

acceptance	debate	heat	persuasion
aggression	defense	hide	pettiness
always there	delay	high energy	positive
ambivalence	destructive	honesty	possibility
anger	differences	hostility	problem solving
angst	different opinion	hurt feelings	progress
annoying	difficult	impediment	relationships
anxiety	disagreement	inevitable	relief
anxious	disappointment	injury	resentment
argue	discomfort	innovation	resignation
assertiveness	discontent	instigator	resolution
attitude	disharmony	intense	retaliation
avoid	disruptive	interesting	revealing
avoidance	disturbing	interpersonal	right/wrong
balance	disunity	intimidating	risk
banter	diversity	irritate	risky
barriers	draining	justice	rough
battle	dynamic	leadership	run from
beneficial	educate	learning	sad
best solutions	elevate	legitimacy	scary
bogged down	emotional	liberating	searching
bring it on	end	listening	signal
build up	energizing	loss of control	solution
calm	engagement	mad	status quo
cautious	enlightening	manageable	stimulating
challenge	equality	messy	stressful
change	essential	misreading	style
chaos	exciting	misunderstanding	success
collaboration	exhausting	mobilizing	synergy
comfort zone	fascinating	natural	tension
communication	favoritism	necessary	tough
compatible	fear	needs	tricky
complex	fearful	negotiation	trust
confrontation	fight	non-conformity	turmoil
confusion	focus	obstinacy	unavoidable
control	freak-out	opportunity	uncertainty
constructive	fruitless	out of control	uncomfortable
conundrum	frustration	pain	uncooperative
costly	fun	painful	understanding
courage	growth	peace	violence
creative tension	grueling	perception	withdraw
creativity	harmony	personality	yelling
curious	hate	perspective	

conflict and the changes and challenges it will bring to our lives. The challenge of having to address the conflict and its emotional consequences can be frightening because our experience has told us this can be frustrating and stressful (Mayer, 2000). These feelings are natural, but they do not tell the entire story of conflict.

Perhaps more interesting are the number of terms that suggest potentially positive elements of conflict: *best solutions, creativity, dynamic, energizing,* and *enlightening.* Did any of those or similar terms occur to you? These may not come to mind as quickly because it takes work to break through the tensions associated with the negative aspects of conflict and reach more positive results. Yet they also give hope to the idea that differences can be resolved and that managing conflict can create positive outcomes for individuals and organizations. If we are able to manage our emotions and behaviors while dealing with differences, we can use the differences to creatively explore alternative approaches to solving problems and possibly find new and better solutions. We can also build stronger relationships that can help us work together more effectively in the future.

Inevitability

Given our definition, it becomes clear that we will face conflict on a regular basis. At both work and home, we have ongoing interdependent relationships with others, and at times we have apparently incompatible differences with them. Yet it is fascinating the number of times we run into people who say about their organizations, "We don't have conflict here." On closer examination, what they often mean is, "We avoid dealing with conflict here." So if conflict is inevitable, what does that mean for people? It largely depends on how they think and feel about conflict. Rather than try to avoid the inevitable, we recommend developing approaches that lessen the potentially harmful effects of conflict. These same approaches can unlock opportunities for solving problems and improving relationships. To do this, it is important to understand something about the life cycle of conflict.

Conflict as a Process

What happens when interdependent people with apparently in-compatible interests interact with one another? How does conflict get started in the first place, and how does it unfold? Over the past several decades, a great deal of research has assisted in uncovering the processes behind conflict. The research has led to the development of a number of theories and models to describe conflict; not surprisingly, many of these have much in common.

In our programs, we use different models to help answer these questions and describe the processes involved. Our core model is called the Dynamic Conflict Model, which is presented graphically in Figure 2.1 (Capobianco, Davis, and Kraus, 2001). This model looks at conflict as a process that unfolds over time, and it explores what triggers conflict in the first place. It also considers how people

Figure 2.1. Dynamic Conflict Model

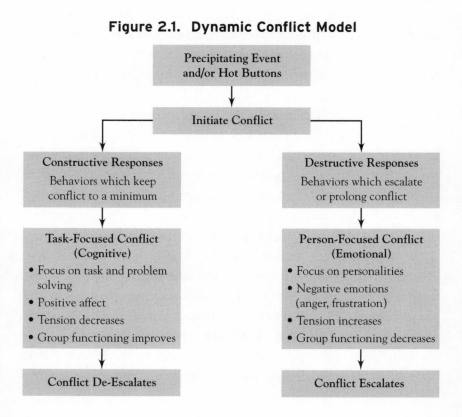

respond to conflict and how different types of responses affect the way in which conflict unfolds. The model focuses on behaviors in order to help people understand how their responses can help or hinder the resolution of the problems and tensions associated with the conflict.

Types of Conflict

The Dynamic Conflict Model relies in part on earlier research that differentiated conflict into two types (Amason, 1996). One type, referred to as *Cognitive Conflict*, focuses more on tasks and problem solving. This is the type of conflict that occurs when people debate ideas. There may appear to be incompatible differences, but the focus remains primarily on ideas, not on people. It could occur when scientists and engineers are arguing vigorously over what approaches to take to solve a problem, lawyers are debating which causes of action to use in an upcoming lawsuit, or managers are at odds over the best strategy to use to address a new business problem.

When the focus is on problem solving, arguments may get quite spirited, but the emotional tone will remain neutral or even positive. The parties may argue vigorously for their positions, but at midday they can go out for lunch together compatibly before returning for more debate. This type of conflict often leads to the creativity, energy, and best solutions our participants identified when they listed positive terms describing conflict. It can also lead to higher productivity because not only can they come up with better solutions to the problem at hand but can also strengthen working relationships that will help them resolve problems in the future.

A second type of conflict, *Affective Conflict*, epitomizes the negative terms that our participants used to describe conflict. Here, the focus is on blaming people or proving that the other person is wrong rather than trying to solve the problem. When differences appear, people think they are right and the other person is wrong. Of course, the other person thinks he or she is right and we are wrong. When people feel threatened, it is easy to fall into this type of personality-focused conflict. It can heat up quickly and is typically associated with a negative emotional tone and ongoing tensions. It also leads to productivity problems because it causes stress and can lead to poorer morale, bad decision making, and other conflict costs described in Chapter One.

A summary of some of the outcomes of these two types of conflict is shown in Table 2.1 (Capobianco, Davis, and Kraus, 2004). Those who seek to obtain the potential benefits of conflict have to engage it and work cooperatively with the other person. The potential downsides stem from attacking people instead of the problem or avoiding the issue altogether. In terms of the latter, one thing is clear: conflict does not go away just because someone avoids it, and neither do the problems it causes.

Table 2.1 Potential Consequences of Conflict

Potential Benefits	*Potential Costs*
• Stimulates creativity and problem solving	• Produces poor quality decisions
• Fosters teamwork and improves social relationships	• Poisons relationships and workplace with misunderstanding and distrust
• Encourages listening and perspective taking	• Disrupts self, others and workplace
• Promotes reflective thinking and open communication	• Causes anger, fear, defensiveness, negativity, hurt, and embarrassment
• Yields information about people and situations	• Detrimental to building lasting relationships
• Signals that changes are necessary in relationships or the organization	• Inhibits open communication
• Provides the means for expressing emotions which can ultimately clear the air and reduce tension	• Lessens joint and individual outcomes
	• Instigates aggression and retaliation
	• Harms reputations
	• Derails careers

Conflict Triggers

The Dynamic Conflict Model uses a fire analogy to describe conflict. It first considers what kind of sparks can get conflict started. One way it can be initiated is by a precipitating event. This usually happens when someone says or does something that causes us to believe that their interests, goals, principles, or feelings are incompatible with and threatening to our own. When this happens, it can set into motion a cascade of events.

Think about when someone said something to you that led to a conflict. Can you remember your initial thoughts about what was going on? It isn't easy because these types of situations can move very quickly. If you can, remember your thoughts about the other person's motives. Did they turn out to be correct, or were there misunderstandings?

Our initial attribution of the other person's motives is often off the mark, as we'll see in the next chapter. For now, the key is that there is an attribution of bad motives that almost instantly leads to the arousal of emotions—typically anger or fear. When emotions start to boil up, we are faced with a question of what we should do with these emotions and how to act on them.

In addition to precipitating events, another kind of spark can launch conflict—something we call *hot buttons*. These are situations or behaviors in others that tend to frustrate or irritate us enough to cause us to overreact in ways we might not if we had cooler heads. Although we will look at these hot buttons in more depth in the next chapter, think for a moment about behaviors in others that irritate you. Is there someone who says or does things that get under your skin? Why is it that this bothers you so? The interesting thing about these hot buttons is that they vary from person to person. Something that may irritate me a great deal might not bother you at all—and vice versa. What is clear is that most people have hot buttons, and when they are pushed, they can lead to anger and frustration.

So whether the initial spark comes from a precipitating event or from hot buttons being pushed, it leads to a situation where emotions are aroused and tensions can grow over perceived incompatibilities. At this point, we face the question of what to do with these feelings. In other words, how do we respond?

Behavioral Responses

The Dynamic Conflict Model suggests that the most important step comes next. When emotions are running high, the key issue is how we respond or behave. Some types of responses tend to enflame or prolong conflict. These destructive behaviors or actions increase the tension that the parties feel and generally prevent effective resolution of the problem. A different set of responses lessens tensions and helps move conflict toward a more constructive resolution.

The question of what constitutes constructive and destructive responses can differ in various cultures. The Dynamic Conflict Model was developed from research focused primarily on a North American business setting, so it tends to favor more direct, active engagement in resolving problems, and its categorization of conflict behaviors demonstrates this. Other cultures prefer more indirect, face-saving approaches to conflict. In this book, we characterize constructive and destructive behaviors in the original manner proposed in the model while acknowledging that specific behaviors constituting constructive and destructive behaviors may change in different cultures.

Destructive Responses.   After conflict has been initiated, people tend to respond in different ways. In Figure 2.1, one path that can be taken involves destructive responses. These are behaviors that tend to enflame or prolong the tensions associated with conflict. They act like throwing gasoline on the initial sparks. They largely fall into the fight-or-flight behaviors associated with conflict. Some of them involve lashing out at or retaliating against the other person; others involve staying away from the conflict or giving in to avoid having to deal with it. For early humans, these responses often contributed to survival when threats arose. Even today, the fight-or-flight instincts prove valuable in settings where one is in danger. The problem is that they do not work well in most modern organizational contexts where our ongoing, interdependent relationships form such an important basis for both success and satisfaction. Using fight-or-flight responses against bosses, coworkers, subordinates, suppliers, and customers does not lead to effective results in the long run or contribute to building stronger working relationships. We will discuss specific destructive and constructive behaviors in the next chapter.

Constructive Responses.   Constructive responses engage with the other person to try to delineate a solution to the problem posed by the differences. They include managing emotions and attitudes to try to avoid destructive responses. More than that, they use approaches that focus on trying to understand the problems caused by differences. This can take a lot of effort because the problems frequently involve more than just factual disputes and include emotions and identity issues (Stone, Patton, and Heen, 1999). It can take a lot of effort to truly understand another person's perspective, particularly when one does not agree with it. Yet once one has a deeper understanding of the nature and reasons underlying the differences, it becomes easier to reframe the problem so that it changes from a matter of "you against me" to "us against the problem." Research related to the Dynamic Conflict Model suggests that some of these constructive behaviors have the highest correlation to effective leadership.

Active and Passive Responses.   Both constructive and destructive behaviors can manifest as active or passive responses. Active responses involve some kind of overt action on the part of a person, whereas a passive response may involve withholding a particular action. An active constructive behavior might be taking the first step to break an impasse; a passive constructive behavior might be taking a time out to let emotions cool down before talking further. Active destructive behaviors are more typically the fight types of responses, like lashing out in anger. Passive destructive behaviors involve more flight types of responses, such as avoiding another person so as not to have to deal with a conflict. Generally we have found that the active types of behaviors, both constructive and destructive, appear to have the greatest impact on how conflict unfolds.

New Responses Can Be Learned.   Although some of these behaviors appear at an early age, the Dynamic Conflict Model suggests that in general, our conflict behaviors are learned. Just relying on gut responses will not ensure that we effectively respond to conflict. It is possible for our gut responses to be affected by emotions like anger and fear, and this can lead us to engage in destructive responses to conflict, which will lead to poorer outcomes. So while leaders often need to trust their responses, a different approach may be needed when dealing with conflict. It becomes important for leaders to understand how they typically respond to conflict in order to learn where they are naturally effective. They also need to understand where they have weak spots, so they can make improvements to strengthen their overall approach. Many times this means learning new behaviors to use in conflict situations. Moreover, leaders need to recognize that everyone in their organization has similar needs. People need to better understand how they respond to conflict so they can improve their behaviors. Although the specifics will differ, essentially everyone can improve how they respond to conflict, and this will lead to more effective management and resolution of conflicts in organizations.

Conflicts Evolve Over Time.   While Figure 2.1 shows a simple division between constructive and destructive behaviors, it turns out that conflict often evolves. Sometimes things go well when people are engaging in constructive behaviors, only for the situation to turn ugly when someone makes a negative comment or behaves destructively. And a conflict that is turning destructive can be rescued if the participants begin to use more constructive behaviors. The Dynamic Conflict Model suggests that the earliest behaviors in a conflict can have the greatest effect on the outcome or direction that conflict takes. It therefore suggests using constructive behaviors at the onset of conflict. This can, of course, be difficult because it is precisely the time when the emotional temperatures are rising. The emotions and associated behaviors of the people can actually feed off one another. As conflict escalates, we turn to another model.

Retaliatory Cycles

The process shown in Figure 2.2 is called the *retaliatory cycle* (Dana, 2005). The first step is the perception of a precipitating event—we see or hear someone do or say something that seems to threaten our interests. The perception is followed closely by the attribution of a motive to the other person. We may see the other person's action as a threat to our own interests. If so, we typically attribute some kind of negative motive to his or her action such as, "He is out to get me" or "She is trying to hog all the resources." This quickly leads to the emotional part of the cycle. The emotion rises not from

Figure 2.2. Retaliatory Cycle

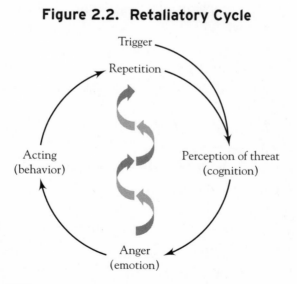

Source: Dana, 2005.

thinking about the issue but from a completely different process—
one that emerges quicker than rational thinking.

People are quickly presented with a situation where they are
feeling an emotion because of something that someone else has said
or done that makes them think he may be threatening their interests. Now they have to make a decision about how they are going
to act and what they are going to do. This is not an easy situation
to be in—but is, in fact, one that is encountered frequently.

If people choose to use constructive responses at this point, the
tension can be reduced, and they can try to find out what is happening. If instead they retaliate, the other person will go through a
similar stage, leading him to the same decision about how to respond. If the response is destructive, the cycle heats up. Sometimes
the cycle is portrayed as a spiral: with each turn, the overall intensity of the emotions escalates and the difficulty of cooling the situation increases (Wilmot and Hocker, 2001).

Consider this situation. Joe was a manager in a technology support group of one of our clients. One day he asked Bill, one of his
technicians, to work overtime on the upcoming weekend. Joe was
surprised when Bill snapped back, "You are always dumping work
on me at the last minute. Why don't you be fair for a change and
ask someone else?" Joe, who felt attacked, responded, "I'm the boss
here, and you'll do what I say!"

This type of escalation happens all the time and frequently goes
much further. In this case, Joe needed help on a project because his
boss had asked him to complete it by Monday. In the past, Joe had
relied on Bill in similar situations and was confident that he would
do a good job. He might even like the overtime because he had not
complained in the past. But this time Bill had plans for the weekend and felt that Joe was taking advantage of him rather than asking another worker. Bill also assumed that Joe had been careless to
wait until the last minute to assign the job and was picking on him.
His response made Bill angry and caused him to snap back at Joe.

Joe felt that Bill was challenging his authority. This made him
angry and led him to overreact. One angry emotion played off another and turned up the heat on the retaliatory cycle, effectively

keeping Joe and Bill from getting to the bottom of what was really happening. In order to understand each other's needs and intentions, they needed to be able to break the retaliatory cycle. Only then could they find ways to take care of their respective interests. Joe, of course, could force the issue, but as we will see later in this chapter, the use of power can often backfire and create resistance.

The retaliatory cycle can be even more harmful if there is a history between the conflict participants that undermines trust and leads them to have deeper suspicions about the other person's motives. Even without such history, it is easy to assume the worst about the other person while assuming the best about one's self.

Roles and Outcomes

A lot of time we look at conflict as a competition: someone wins and the other person loses. It becomes a struggle to make sure that the other person loses so we get what we want. The interchange with the other person essentially consists of hard bargaining and trying to persuade her that our position is the correct one. Power becomes something to be used as leverage to ensure our own "victory." This competitive perspective tends to be associated with the destructive behaviors described by the Dynamic Conflict Model. When conflict becomes a win-or-lose struggle, fight-or-flight responses kick in, and destructive behaviors emerge that enflame conflict.

A very different approach was developed by researchers at the Harvard Negotiation Project. This approach is variously described as negotiating on the merits or principled- or interest-based negotiation. It focuses on understanding the interests of each party and cooperatively developing options that "enlarge the pie" before trying to decide how to divide it (Fisher, Ury, and Patton, 1991). This value creation process changes the perspective from a zero-sum game to a win-win or "both-gain" scenario. It is conceptually consistent with the Dynamic Conflict Model. Many of the constructive behaviors found in the latter are precisely those used to understand the interests of the people involved in the conflict and then create solutions that benefit all parties. It effectively enables people to reframe conflict to be more of a cooperative problem-solving effort and less of a competitive contest.

The Role of Power in Conflict

Since leaders are often in roles of power in their own organizations, it is natural to inquire about how power affects the process of conflict. The subject is actually quite complex and can involve exploring sources of power, how it is used, and the relational aspects of it. We'll focus here on one relational aspect of power: how it is used either against or in cooperation with others.

When one party has or acquires more power than another in a conflict, he may choose to use it to force a solution that favors him. Although this approach can achieve short-term objectives, a potential problem lies in alienating people who will be needed to implement the solution or from whom cooperation will be needed in the future. It may sometimes be necessary to use power coercively in a particular setting. If, however, a leader becomes dependent on or habituated to a winning-at-all-costs strategy, it can create resentment, alienation, and eventually resistance from those on the losing side. This can lead to lower morale, vandalism, and other actions that lower productivity and increase the need for closer controls (Coleman, 2000).

Power can also be used in more cooperative ways. If one party has more power than someone with whom she is experiencing conflict, she can choose to make sure that it is seen as a mutual problem rather than just a struggle for unilateral victory. By framing the process as a cooperative search for win-win options, she can ensure greater buy-in from the other person. It does not lessen her chances to get what she wants since she is searching for mutually satisfactory approaches. It will enhance her chances of reaching an agreement where the parties are committed to a successful implementation.

Conflict and Culture

The principal models presented in this book are derived from Western views of conflict, principally those found in North America and Northern Europe. They represent cultures that value individualism and appreciate openness, directness, and goal-oriented solutions. Yet much of the rest of the world, including many countries in Asia, the Middle East, Africa, and Latin America, take a more collectivist view of conflict. In these cultures, maintaining harmony and strong relationships is considered just as important as or more important than goal outcomes. Direct criticism and debate may be avoided not only because they do not fit the norms of these cultures, but also because they can pose a threat to relationships (Ting-Toomey and Oetzel, 2001). As the world grows smaller and people from different cultures interact with one another, conflict between them will occur with increasing frequency. In these cases, conflict competent leaders will seek to learn more concerning other cultures' approaches to conflict. They will also work at being mindful of these differences and try to understand not only the other person's interests but also how that person deals with conflict (LeBaron, 2003; Ting-Toomey and Oetzal, 2001).

Most leaders work in organizations that are made up of people from different cultural backgrounds or deal with people from varying cultures. As a consequence, it will be increasingly important for them to ensure that their organizations' conflict management training programs incorporate intercultural components.

Understanding Your Role in Conflict

We've looked at some of the basic elements of conflict and have explored how people view it. A conflict competent leader develops an understanding of these elements in order to cultivate a deeper appreciation about how our perceptions, emotions, and behaviors affect the manner in which conflict unfolds. It is not enough, though, just to understand the concepts. A second step is to become aware of how our own personal preferences and approaches differ from those of others and reflect on how they can become a source for conflict or a basis for its resolution. This includes looking at what triggers conflict, as well as how we respond to it. Chapter Three explores this topic in more depth.

3

SELF-AWARENESS, SELF-CONTROL

First keep the peace within yourself, then you can
also bring peace to others.

—*Thomas à Kempis*

Self-awareness plays a crucial role in our leadership development programs. We believe that leaders need to know more about their own personalities, preferences, and styles in order to better understand why they behave in certain ways. We use a model developed by the Center for Creative Leadership known as ACS, which stands for Assessment, Challenge, and Support. Assessment helps clarify changes that may be needed to improve leadership effectiveness. Challenge provides the opportunity for experimentation and practice to make changes. Support helps confirm and clarify lessons learned (McCauley, Moxley, and Van Velsor, 1998).

In this chapter, we address the assessment component of the ACS model. Assessment assists people in becoming more aware of themselves. It goes beyond just understanding oneself, though. It includes looking at how one interacts with people who have different preferences and styles from oneself. Participants in our programs are often surprised to discover how easily these differences can spark conflict. We also help them look at what kinds of behaviors in others might trigger conflict for them. Finally, we help them explore how they respond when they are faced with conflict. Sometimes their self-awareness is enhanced by getting feedback from companions in the program. Other times it comes from the use of assessment instruments.

In addition to self-awareness, leaders need to cultivate self-control so they can respond in ways that are best suited to the situation. Losing one's cool can be a problem for anyone, but when a leader loses control, the consequences for the organization can be disastrous. Self-awareness and self-control are key elements in the creation of conflict competent leaders.

Self-Awareness

In the context of conflict, leaders need to become aware of how and where conflicts arise for them, how they might cause conflicts, and how they respond emotionally and behaviorally in a conflict. Better self-awareness enables leaders to learn how they deal with conflict and helps make sure that they use behaviors that minimize the harmful effects of conflict.

Differences

Our definition of *conflict* sees differences as being a key element of conflict. Everyone is aware of common ways in which they differ from other people. These could be different thoughts about strategic directions or tactics, perceptions about resource allocations, and opinions on organizational structure and individual responsibility. How do these arise?

Some may come from people having different amounts of information or understanding about a problem. Some can stem from naturally competing interests—departments competing for resources or individuals competing for promotions, for example. In many cases, though, the differences arise from people's different personalities, preferences, and styles. Too often these lead to conflict because of misunderstandings. The conflict competent leader understands his or her own styles and preferences, recognizes potential strengths and weaknesses related to them, appreciates that other people can have different ones, and works to make these differences a source of opportunity rather than conflict.

Many leaders have taken the Meyers-Briggs Type Indicator (MBTI)—some perhaps many times. Most people who come to our programs already know whether they are an ISTJ, ENTP, or some other type. They may have reflected on their specific type and have read about the characteristics of that type in specific contexts. They have generally thought less about how differences in types might lead to conflict.

The MBTI looks at four basic set of preferences: Extroversion-Introversion (where you focus your attention), Sensing-Intuition (how you acquire information), Thinking-Feeling (how you make decisions), and Judging-Perceiving (orientation to the outer world). How could different preferences in these areas lead to conflict? Anyone who remembers dealing with someone with a different type may have experienced the kinds of frustrations that can spark conflict. Many times when people experience something different, their first impulse is to see their way as the right way and the other person's way as wrong.

Introverts, who prefer quieter working environments, might find extroverts, who prefer more interaction, to be disruptive. If the differences are too great, the level of disruption may itself cause conflict. People with a Sensing preference appreciate detail and could be frustrated when people with an Intuitive preference give more big-picture directions or feedback. Someone with a Feeling preference may become upset by a colleague with a Thinking preference who criticizes without also showing appreciation. A person with a Judging preference will want to carefully plan out a project, while a colleague with a Perceiving preference may prefer to let things evolve with less structure. This could lead to conflict if they are on the same team. Irritations like these can run in both directions and can lead to conflict (Van Sant, 2003).

There are no right or wrong preferences; moreover, people are not always bound to act in line with their preferences. It is helpful to recognize our own preferences and acknowledge that other people's may vary from these. If you sense friction with someone, stop for a moment to consider whether it may be stemming from these different preferences. If so, you may want to reach out in a manner that acknowledges the other's preferences and find a way to communicate effectively with him or her.

A conflict competent leader will recognize that these differences can be the source of organizational strength. It is helpful to have the flexibility that comes from having some people who work well with details (Sensing preference) and others who prefer to look for big-picture themes and principles (Intuitive preference). The key for the conflict competent leader is to value differences and make sure that others in the organization do, too. Once the differences are valued, it becomes easier to overcome the frustrations and use the strengths inherent in having diversity of preferences.

Another instrument we use in some of our leadership and conflict management programs, the Kirton Adaption Innovation Inventory, looks at how people approach problem solving and manage change (Kirton, 2003). It is based on a model that suggests people have different cognitive styles that are distinguished from their problem-solving capacity. Whereas capacity relates to how smart or effective someone may be at problem solving, style looks at the preferred manner in which he or she goes about the task. Some people are seen as having a more adaptive style. They prefer to work within an established set of rules or paradigm. They seek to make things better by making incremental improvements to the current system, and they prefer to work in harmony with others while doing this. They tend to work efficiently, and they come up with fewer but more relevant ideas for solving a problem.

This model also describes an innovative style. People with this style come up with lots of ideas, many of which may not be relevant or practical. Innovators are less tied to the current way of doing things and are much less concerned about bending or breaking the rules than adaptors. They are also less concerned about following procedures and maintaining harmony with others while engaged in problem solving.

These differences in styles can create friction and conflict within teams. Adaptors often see people who are more innovative as disruptive, impractical risk-takers. Innovators see adaptors as unimaginative, boring, stick-in-the-mud thinkers. Neither understands the other very well, and they usually see each other's approaches as wrong. It is easy to see how these perceptions can cause conflict to arise whenever they are called on to solve problems together.

In some ways, it is much easier to manage a team if all of the members have similar styles. This ease of management comes with a cost. While the team members can probably do a great job solving problems that are suited to their style, they will have difficulty addressing problems that are better handled by a different style.

From a leadership perspective, having diversity among problem-solving styles brings flexibility and adaptability. The effective leader appreciates diversity for the value it brings and makes sure to recruit for it. Managing this diversity creates other challenges. It requires working with team members to help them tolerate and eventually appreciate the value that people with different styles bring to the team. While the differences may still lead to occasional conflicts, they become more manageable and less divisive.

So conflict competent leaders explore personal styles and preferences that can cause conflict between them and others. In addition, they appreciate how these characteristics may differ from those of other people and how these differences can lead to conflict, as well as how they can add value. The key becomes effective management of this diversity.

In addition to appreciating differences, it is important for conflict competent leaders to understand what kinds of situations and behaviors in others may trigger conflict for them.

Triggers

We find it important to help clients understand what triggers conflict for them. Differences alone are not enough to do so.

One aspect of the Dynamic Conflict Model that we use in our leadership programs focuses on hot buttons—situations or behaviors that can upset individuals enough to cause them to overreact in destructive ways. Although there are innumerable behaviors in others that could irritate people, the model focuses on nine behaviors that seem to be particularly prevalent or disturbing in workplace settings:

- Unreliable—when people miss deadlines or cannot be counted on
- Overly analytical—when people focus too much on minor issues or are perfectionists
- Unappreciative—when people fail to give credit to others or seldom praise good performance
- Aloof—when people isolate themselves, do not seek input, or are hard to approach
- Micro-managing—when people constantly monitor and check up on the work of others
- Self-centered—when people believe they are always correct or care only about themselves
- Abrasive—when people are arrogant, sarcastic, and demeaning
- Untrustworthy—when people exploit others, take undeserved credit, or cannot be trusted
- Hostile—when people lose their tempers, become angry, or yell at others

The Dynamic Conflict Model is supported by an assessment instrument, the Conflict Dynamics Profile (CDP) (Capobianco, Davis, and Kraus, 1999). We use the CDP to measure people's hot buttons and the behaviors they use when faced with conflict in the workplace. When they take the CDP, people answer a series of questions about how irritating the hot button behaviors are for them. Their answers are compared with those of thousands of other people who have taken the instrument to determine whether their reactivity to a particular hot button is higher than, lower than, or similar to others. Figure 3.1 shows a graph from the CDP that displays measures of hot buttons. The results in the figure show a person who is quite irritated when dealing with people who behave in self-centered ways.

Figure 3.1. Measures of Hot Buttons

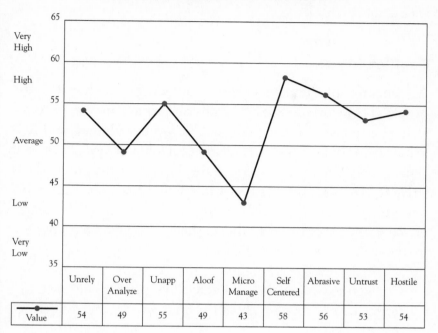

	Unrely	Over Analyze	Unapp	Aloof	Micro Manage	Self Centered	Abrasive	Untrust	Hostile
Value	54	49	55	49	43	58	56	53	54

Note: Lower numbers are more desirable.

Source: Capobianco, Davis, and Kraus, 1999.

Understanding our own hot buttons can help us avoid getting thrown off balance. We will be more aware when someone's behavior becomes irritating so we can cool down before saying or doing something we might later regret (a sample hot button survey is available to try online at www.conflictdynamics.org/hb.php).

Responses to Conflict

Understanding differences and triggers helps explain how conflicts get started. The next step is to understand how to approach conflict once it has begun. The traditional approach to assessing these responses was to look at general styles that people use when dealing with conflict, which provide a high-level look at behaviors. Newer instruments begin to explore more specific behavioral responses to conflict. Both can be used to help better understand how to deal with conflict.

Conflict Styles

A number of instruments measure conflict styles. They describe people's behaviors along two dimensions, which are variously described as concern for self–concern for other (Thomas and Kilmann, 1974) or importance of relationship–importance of outcome (Hiam, 1999). All of them look at the degree to which individuals strive to get their own needs met in relation to the amount of interest they have in the other person's needs being met. The degree of importance of one or the other of these concerns determines the individual's preferred conflict style:

- Competing—high levels of interest in satisfying one's own interest and low concern about the other person's needs (defeat the other)
- Avoiding—low level of interest in meeting the needs of either person (prefers not to deal with the issue)
- Accommodating—low level of concern about meeting one's own needs and high level of interest in meeting the other's needs (give in to the other)
- Compromising—midlevel interest in the needs of both parties (split the difference)
- Collaborating—high level of interest in meeting both parties' needs (try for a win-win or both-gain solution)

As with many other measures, it is helpful not only to discover our own style but to examine its pros and cons, which are often related to particular situations. While many people advocate the benefits of a collaborative style, it might not be appropriate in situations with an untrustworthy opponent. Likewise, an avoiding style tends not to help resolve conflicts, but sometimes it may be the best approach, at least temporarily, when safety is an issue. So no one style is always good or always bad. Each must be viewed in context. If your preferred style does not work well for a specific situation, then you are not bound to it. You can behave in other ways that are not characteristic of your style; it may just take more effort to do so. Styles should also be viewed in relation to the other people in the conflict. If you become aware of another person's style, you may be able to reach out to her more effectively by adapting your behaviors in a way that she can better understand.

A different approach to conflict styles is found in the Intercultural Conflict Style Inventory (ICSI) (Hammer, 2003). This instrument examines two dimensions: the degree to which people use direct versus indirect communication styles and whether they use emotionally expressive or restrained approaches when dealing with conflict. Our earlier discussions of culture touched on differences between individualistic and collectivist cultures. In the case of the ICSI, individualistic cultures tend to favor more direct communications approaches where a person means what he or she says. Collectivist cultures prefer to use indirect approaches where issues are not addressed head on in order to preserve relationship harmony.

The emotional domain of the ICSI focuses on how people from different cultures handle their emotions when dealing with others about conflict. Expressive cultures value sharing emotions and build trust and credibility in this way. Cultures that use emotional restraint internalize feelings and view the use of self-control as a means to avoiding hurting others' feelings.

The combinations of these dimensions (direct/indirect and expressive/restrained) create four separate, intercultural conflict styles. The ICSI characterizes people who are direct and emotionally restrained as having a *discussion style*. This approach is typical of people in North America and northern Europe and reflects the characterization of constructive and destructive behaviors found in the Dynamic Conflict Model.

People who use direct communications and are emotionally expressive are said to have an *engagement style*. This style is said to be common among people in a number of southern European countries as well as among African Americans. The combination of indirect communications and an emotionally expressive style is termed a *dynamic approach* and is found among a number of Middle Eastern cultures. Finally, people who use indirect communication and a restrained emotional approach are characterized as having an *accommodating style*. This style is prevalent among people in collectivist cultures, particularly in Asia (Hammer, 2005).

Appreciating your own intercultural conflict style can help you understand more about your own approaches but also how these differ from those of other people. None of the styles is right or wrong, but the differences among them can cause misunderstandings about what other people are doing and why they are approaching conflict so differently. Knowing more about the different styles and how others perceive them can help you maintain your balance when dealing with someone who has a different style. It can also keep these differences from exacerbating the underlying conflict.

Style measures provide a helpful, high-level overview of how each of us approaches conflict. As we have seen, this can provide a valuable perspective on how a person is likely to approach conflict. Yet the behaviors measured in the style approaches are often so broad that it is difficult to change them. This led to the development of assessments that look at more specific behaviors people use when they are facing conflict.

Behaviors

The Dynamic Conflict Model that we use in our leadership programs takes an approach that focuses on specific behaviors that people engage in when responding to conflict (Capobianco, Davis, and Kraus, 2004). This model differentiates constructive and destructive behaviors. It also divides both types into active and passive responses. In essence it creates four categories of conflict behaviors: Active Constructive, Passive Constructive, Active Destructive, and Passive Destructive. Figure 3.2 shows these four categories, together with specific behaviors that the model ascribes to each.

Figure 3.2. Responses to Conflict

	Constructive	Destructive
Active	Perspective Taking Creating Solutions Expressing Emotions Reaching Out	Winning at All Costs Displaying Anger Demeaning Others Retaliating
Passive	Reflective Thinking Delay Responding Adapting	Avoiding Yielding Hiding Emotions Self-Criticizing

Active Constructive Behaviors. The Active Constructive behaviors involve some overt action on the part of a person and typically reduce the tension associated with conflict. The behaviors are Perspective Taking, Creating Solutions, Expressing Emotions, and Reaching Out.

Perspective Taking means trying to understand the other person's point of view—walking in his shoes. In our experience, it is perhaps the most powerful of the constructive behaviors. By genuinely listening to the other person in a conflict context, we can learn more about the full nature of the problem. Often we think we understand an issue, but too often this ends up meaning that we know the issue from our own perspective and believe that we are right. By taking the time to understand where the other person is coming from, we can clarify misunderstandings and gain a clearer picture of what is really at issue. In addition, listening to the other person gives her a chance to feel heard and perhaps even to vent, which leads to a catharsis that can lessen tensions.

Creating Solutions means working with the other person to come up with options for successfully resolving a problem as opposed to continually focusing on who is to blame. Craig's wife, Kathy, gives a good analogy that typifies this behavior. She says that when they are having an argument, "they can stand on opposite sides of a fence from one another and lob accusations back and forth or they can choose to stand on the same side of the fence, put the problem on the other side, and work together to solve it."

Expressing Emotions concerns responding to conflict by openly and honestly sharing feelings. We often get resistance concerning this behavior since many people feel that it is inappropriate to talk about emotions in the workplace. When we ask whether they experience emotions related to conflict, the answer is invariably yes—usually coupled with a reiteration that it is not something that can be talked about at work, though. Our next question is, "Can you really hold the emotion totally inside?" Most people agree that this is not so easy and that often their pent-up emotions will either leak out as some kind of demeaning remark or will come gushing out in a more explosive form. The essence of Expressing Emotions is to share them in a more forthright manner so others do not misunderstand them and thus create further problems. Of course, there is a time and place issue associated with Expressing Emotions: when tempers are running hot, it may well be best to wait until things cool down before sharing one's feelings.

When people engage in *Reaching Out*, they take the first steps to break a deadlock or try to make amends. It takes courage to reach out because it is certainly possible for the overture to be met with rejection. At the same time, the use of conciliatory gestures, such as apologizing when appropriate, can have a tremendous impact on opening up communications and enabling people to work on solving a problem on which they had become entrenched.

Research has demonstrated that these Active Constructive behaviors are the ones most strongly correlated with perceived leadership effectiveness. The study showed that people who use higher levels of Perspective Taking, Creating Solutions, Expressing Emotions, and Reaching Out were seen by their bosses, peers, and subordinates as being more effective leaders and more suitable for promotion (Capobianco, Davis, and Kraus, 2005).

One of the most powerful Active Constructive responses is Perspective Taking. Many managers who come to our programs are quite good at decision making, and sometimes it is more difficult for them to engage in Perspective Taking—understanding the concerns of others. Fran was an extremely experienced manager who knew her retail business inside and out. Many times she would not wait for her employees to finish their questions before she told them how they should handle the situation. Given her experience, her answers were usually right, but by not taking time to understand the perspectives of her employees better, she was causing friction. They felt unheard and disrespected. On reflection, Fran felt she needed to encourage her employees to begin to think for themselves even if it took some extra time and meant having to listen to some naive approaches at first. She figured that the only way for the employees to develop their own problem-solving skills was to hear them out. By using this Active Constructive response, she was able to lessen tension and participate in her employees' growth.

Passive Constructive Behaviors. The Passive Constructive behaviors—Reflective Thinking, Delay Responding, and Adapting—involve withholding actions and serve to reduce tensions and negative outcomes of conflict.

Reflective Thinking means weighing the pros and cons of a particular situation to consider the best resolution to a problem. It is closely associated with Perspective Taking since it is difficult to adequately weigh the pros and cons of various approaches without appreciating the issues and needs of both sides.

Delay Responding becomes particularly important for people whose emotions are easily aroused and makes use of calling a time-out to let the situation calm down before further interactions. It differs from avoiding a conflict in that the intention is to return to discussions when emotions have cooled and the parties are better able to listen to one another.

Adapting behavior involves staying flexible and trying to make the best out of a situation. Not every conflict can be solved in a totally satisfactory manner, but those who are adaptable can make adjustments to ensure that the solution does not cause unnecessary problems in the future. It can also mean adopting a positive attitude toward the conflict such as, "I'm confident that we can find a way to make things work or at least to maintain a good working relationship in the future." This type of positive attitude can be helpful when dealing with difficult subjects.

Although the Passive Constructive behaviors are not as strongly correlated with leadership effectiveness as the Active Constructive responses, they nevertheless show positive correlations to it and can be seen as behaviors that more effective leaders use in addressing conflict.

For people who experience strong emotions around conflict, the Passive Constructive behavior of Delay Responding can be crucial. Mike, a manager in one of our client companies, had a short fuse. When confronted with conflict, he quickly got angry and acted out by shouting and being sarcastic. Although he was regarded as technically competent, his outbursts became his trademark and began to jeopardize his career. Eventually Mike resolved to try to let conflicts cool down first before talking. He asked others to tell him when he began acting out his anger. In time, he was able to slow down long enough to let the heat of the moment pass. Mike became effective in dealing with conflict, and it improved his reputation.

Active Destructive Behaviors. The Active Destructive behaviors are ways of responding that require effort on the part of an individual and tend to enflame or prolong conflict. They are Winning at All Costs, Displaying Anger, Demeaning Others, and Retaliating.

In *Winning at All Costs*, the key emphasis is on the "at all costs" element. There is nothing wrong with winning, but it can become a problem for those who are so focused on the goal that they win the battle but lose the war. If the entire focus becomes winning, it can lead to behaviors that damage ongoing working relationships, which are required to be able to carry on effective collaboration in the future.

Displaying Anger is distinguished from the constructive behavior of Expressing Emotions by both its harshness and its typical focus on the other person. It often occurs when emotions are aroused, and the individual is unable to control the impulse to lash out and blame the other person for the problem. The angry display may feel good at the moment, but it can evoke negative responses from the person who is its target and escalate conflict.

People who engage in *Demeaning Others* are often surprised when they learn that they use sarcasm or otherwise act in ways that devalue the other person with whom they are having a conflict. This behavior does not require conscious intent to put down the other person; rather, it looks at the effects that the behavior has on others. It is one way that emotions can leak out if they are not dealt with in open and honest communications.

Retaliating behavior is another response that can occur because people do not deal openly with their emotions. Retaliating and the other Active Destructive behaviors are quite toxic and can disrupt personal relationships for a long time. People do not forget when someone retaliates against or demeans them.

Active Destructive behaviors are negatively correlated with leadership effectiveness: people who use them are not seen as effective leaders. Moreover, research shows that these destructive behaviors have negative effects on relationship satisfaction in couples (Gottman and Levenson, 1992). The Active Destructive behaviors do not play out well at work or at home.

We find that many times when people are unable to share their feelings openly and honestly with others, they let those emotions build up. Eventually they leak out as Active Destructive behaviors like Demeaning Others or Retaliating. It is as though the emotions reach a point where they can no longer be contained and they have to find an escape. When they are not shared directly, they find another behavioral outlet, which is often confusing and irritating to other people.

Passive Destructive Behaviors.   Passive Destructive behaviors refer to responses that involve a withholding of particular actions and escalate tensions associated with conflict. In terms of fight-or-flight responses, these constitute flight. The four Passive Destructive behaviors are Avoiding, Yielding, Hiding Emotions, and Self-Criticizing.

People who use *Avoiding* responses try to stay away from the other person and act aloof because they do not want to deal with the conflict. The trouble is that avoiding a conflict does not make it go away. Rather, it tends to fester and flare up again when another aggravating circumstance occurs.

Yielding means giving in to another person in order to avoid having to deal with conflict. Sometimes people ask, "Doesn't it make sense to yield sometimes? I'll give in on something that isn't as important to me, and I'll get something in return from the other side." The answer to this is yes. But the real issue is how often people engage in this kind of behavior. If they do it once in awhile, it may be more of a tactical expression. If they do it frequently, then it is more likely that they are yielding to avoid having to deal with conflict. When this is the case, it can create a defeatist sense in the person. It can also result in poorer results for the organization: if a person gives in just to avoid conflict and that person's idea is actually better than that of the other person, the organization suffers.

Hiding Emotions is related to the constructive response of Expressing Emotions, but in this case, the individual conceals his or her true emotions even though he or she may feel upset. Whereas Expressing Emotions involves openly and honestly sharing feeling, Hiding Emotions involves working at keeping emotions inside and not showing them to other people.

Self-Criticizing behaviors can sap the energy of those who use them and the focus they need to move on after conflict ends. It is one thing to learn from mistakes from time to time. This can clearly be helpful so that we are more effective in future conflicts. When Self-Criticizing happens frequently, it often becomes a self-defeating drain on one's energy.

The Passive Destructive behaviors are also negatively correlated with perceived leadership effectiveness, although less strongly than the Active Destructive behaviors are with one exception. The Passive Destructive behavior of Avoiding has a higher negative correlation from the viewpoint of bosses. In other words, those in charge think that avoiding conflict is not a trait of effective leaders.

Many people prefer to avoid conflict. Conflict can be unnerving and the emotions associated with it messy. Paul, the president of a medium-sized financial services company, disliked conflict. His actions created an unspoken motto for his company, "No Conflict Here!" This, of course, actually translated to, "Our conflict goes underground and festers." Eventually a neglected conflict blew up in a class action lawsuit involving discrimination claims. When asked, people in the company admitted they knew about the problems, but no one would bring them up until things reached a point of no return.

So, in general, the research on conflict behaviors and leadership suggests that effective leaders should engage rather than avoid conflict. They should particularly use Active Constructive behaviors to reach out to the other person, work on understanding the other person's interests, share their own feelings about the conflict, and reframe the conflict so that all parties can work cooperatively to solve it.

Measuring Behaviors: Conflict Dynamics Profile. One version of the CDP is known as a 360-degree or multirater instrument. It measures how a person sees himself or herself responding to conflict, and it compares this response with how this person's boss, peers, and subordinates see that individual. This instrument uses questionnaires that ask people how often individuals engage in particular actions that are related to the various behaviors. Their frequency of use of the behaviors is compared to thousands of others who have taken the instrument, and the results are then plotted to show whether they use the behaviors more often, less often, or about average when compared with other people.

Figures 3.3 and 3.4 show graphs from a sample CDP report that measures constructive and destructive behaviors. They show the individual's self-rating on the various behaviors described, as well as the ratings of that person by respondents. This and similar graphs are used to diagnose both constructive and destructive behaviors where the person is already effective, as well as those that could be

Figure 3.3. Sample CDP Report Measuring Constructive Responses

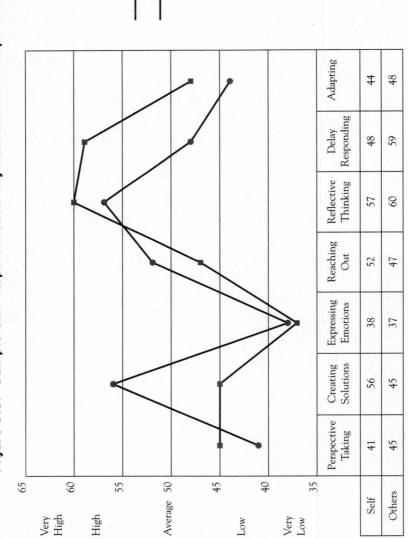

	Perspective Taking	Creating Solutions	Expressing Emotions	Reaching Out	Reflective Thinking	Delay Responding	Adapting
Self	41	56	38	52	57	48	44
Others	45	45	37	47	60	59	48

Note: Higher numbers are more desirable.

Figure 3.4. Sample CDP Report Measuring Destructive Responses

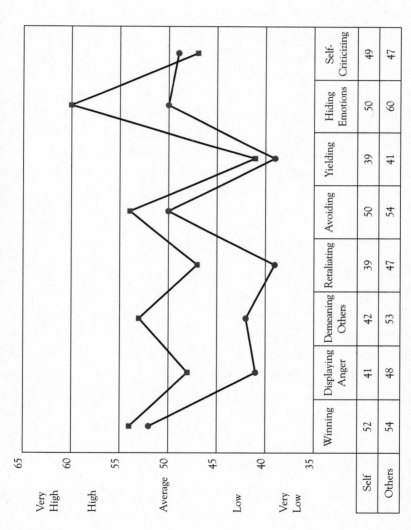

	Winning	Displaying Anger	Demeaning Others	Retaliating	Avoiding	Yielding	Hiding Emotions	Self-Criticizing
Self	52	41	42	39	50	39	50	49
Others	54	48	53	47	54	41	60	47

Note: Lower numbers are more desirable.

improved. It also helps point out potential blind spots where the perspectives of the individual and the respondents are different.

For example, in Figure 3.3, the individual is seen as engaging in higher levels of Reflective Thinking, a potential strength, whereas the scores for Expressing Emotions fall in the very low range, suggesting a possible area for development. In Figure 3.4 we see a potential blind spot on Demeaning Others, where the individual rates himself or herself in the low range but the other respondents see that person on the border of the high range, suggesting that this could be a problem area.

The conflict competent leader makes efforts to better understand his or her own views, approaches, and responses to conflict. This may mean attending programs in conflict management, taking assessment instruments, and working with an executive coach. It is not enough to tell others to do these things. The leader needs to take these steps for himself or herself. When others see the leader doing this, it will become easier to encourage them to do so as well.

Self-Control

Conflict competent leaders need to be self-aware about how conflict arises for them and how they respond to it. It takes more than that, though. Being able to have control over their emotional responses and behaviors is equally important. In Chapter Two, we looked at the retaliatory cycle of conflict and saw how emotions play a key role in it. We are going to take a closer look at parts of the cycle and see why a situation can get out of control and what can be done about it.

Perception and Attribution

The retaliatory cycle starts when we perceive that someone else says or does something that might be harmful to our own interests. It is certainly possible for the perception itself to be faulty—notice, for instance, the notorious fallibility of eyewitness testimony. Even if our own perception is accurate, there is still the problem of imputing motive related to the other person's actions. This attribution of motive often occurs quickly, and the speculative assumptions that accompany it are often incorrect.

The kind of motive a person attributes tends to be related to things such as the degree of control he believes the other person had over her actions, whether he believes that her actions were intentional, and his own history with and trust of her. This process is complicated by attribution errors that include a tendency to infer a bad motive related to the other person's character, known as *accuser bias*. At the same time, he sees his own motives more favorably and treats his own failings as more related to circumstances that are beyond his control—*bias of the accused*. These biases in the process of attribution can arouse negative emotions particularly when he believes the other person's harmful action was within her control and was caused by some character failing. When these negative feelings occur, he gets angry and feels like striking back; if he does this, he can escalate the retaliatory cycle (Allred, 2000). Once the attribution has been made, we become committed to it and look for evidence to support it (Wiersma, 2006).

Have you ever attributed a motive to someone that turned out to be wrong? When Martha's boss told her that a new person from headquarters would be working with her on the new project, Martha's first thought was that the new person was being put there as a spy. Martha chafed at her boss's lack of confidence in her. When they finally talked, she found out the new person was being placed there to learn from Martha, who was highly respected. If Martha had relied on her initial assumptions, she would have continued to harbor ill feelings.

So what can be done about this problem? The first thing is to recognize that everyone has the tendency toward these accuser and accused biases. Acknowledge that your initial attribution is probably just based on assumptions and speculation and that it is very easy to see the other person's actions in a bad light and your own in a good light. It then becomes easier to slow down and try to find out what is actually behind the other person's actions (Stone, Patton, and Heen, 1999). The constructive behaviors needed to do this are explored in more detail in Chapter Five.

Emotions

In some ways, conflict is all about emotions. We have seen that destructive emotions can arise when people attribute bad motives to other individuals whose words or actions appear to be threatening to their interests. In the retaliatory cycle model, emotions are seen as arising very quickly. How do these emotions emerge, and what can we do about them?

Considerable research has been done to understand the psychological and neurological underpinnings of emotions. Paul Ekman (2003), a leading researcher, suggests that one common source of emotions is our perception that someone or something may seriously affect our own well-being. He believes that we are all constantly monitoring our environment for such threats. This process is accomplished by brain functions he terms *auto-appraisers*, which operate automatically and rapidly. Some of these auto-appraisers appear to be universal among humans and are probably an evolutionary development that serves as a safeguard to our survival. Most people, for instance, wince when something appears to be coming at their head, even without having to think about it. Afterward they feel a sense of fear. Other auto-appraisers seem to be specific to individuals, who may learn them based on their unique life experiences. When these auto-appraisers perceive something that can threaten us or our interests, they can trigger an emotion such as fear or anger within milliseconds without our conscious awareness that this is happening.

Ekman recognizes that emotions can be triggered in other ways, such as remembering or talking about past emotional experiences, but he sees the auto-appraisers as the most common source for emotions. He also notes that auto-appraisers can be wrong. In other words, they can perceive threats that do not actually exist. When they do, they can still trigger emotions. Have you ever been scared by a shape formed by a shadow that turned out to be something completely harmless? Or perhaps more relevant, have you ever been frightened or angered by something someone else said because you thought you heard something that was different from what was actually spoken?

Once an emotion has been triggered, we enter what Ekman calls a *refractory period* when the emotion holds sway over our rationality. Logical persuasion is useless because whatever is said is transformed to justify our own emotion. Let's say that I am really angry at you because I think you cheated me. During the refractory period, your attempts to persuade me otherwise will go for naught because I will twist your logic in a way to support my anger. Obviously this period can be fraught with problems, and research suggests the stronger the intensity of the emotion, the longer the recovery time or refractory period will be (Goleman, 2003).

All of us are constantly on the lookout for possible threats to our own interests. If our auto-appraisers pick something up, then our emotions can be triggered in a way that leaves us unable to rationally reflect on them for a period of time. This makes us susceptible to saying or doing something that we might later regret. We are particularly vulnerable to these forces when the emotional reaction is strong or if we are in a bad mood or under stress. To keep emotions from escalating into a retaliatory cycle requires either lessening the intensity of our triggers and shortening our refractory time or controlling our behavioral responses to our emotions. We will discuss both of these points in the next two sections of this chapter. Before we do that, though, let us first look at one other way to keep destructive emotions from getting the upper hand.

Research has determined that specific structures in the brain are responsible for triggering emotions as well as moderating them. The prefrontal cortex, the portion of the brain related to intelligence, moderates emotions. Interestingly, different parts of the prefrontal cortex are involved with different types of emotions. The right portion experiences greater activation when negative emotions like anger and fear are experienced. The left portion is more activated when positive emotions like happiness and compassion are experienced. It appears that people who have more left side activity and experience more positive emotions tend to have shorter refractory periods and thus better control of their emotions (Goleman, 2003).

This suggests that it is worthwhile to cultivate positive emotions that serve as antidotes to negative ones. This may be accomplished by various means that emphasize positive emotions including the use of reason, the cultivation of empathy and compassion, substituting positive emotions for negative ones, using certain types of contemplative or meditative practices, and picturing oneself in the other person's position (Goleman, 2003).

Negotiation experts Roger Fisher and Daniel Shapiro (2005) have suggested a variation on this approach. Although they applaud the value of cultivating positive emotions in oneself and the other person, they recommend doing so by focusing on what they call core concerns as opposed to thinking in terms of specific emotions. They believe that dealing with emotions can be too complex because there are so many of them, they can be hard to recognize, and they are constantly changing. Fisher and Shapiro instead suggest enhancing positive emotional tone by making sure that five core concerns are managed effectively:

- Appreciation—acknowledging the value of people
- Affiliation—developing connections with another person
- Autonomy—respecting the freedom of people to make decisions
- Status—recognizing the specialty of others
- Role—making sure that people have a clear, meaningful purpose

Addressing these concerns in negotiation and conflict management context will foster positive emotions, which will help lessen the effects of negative ones. Fisher and Shapiro recognize that negative emotions will still arise, but less frequently if the core concerns are addressed. In those cases, they recommend having an emergency plan in place to help cool down the negative emotions as well as investigating what might be behind the trigger and devising an approach to address the source of it.

Cooling Hot Buttons

Some situations or behaviors in others can trigger stronger reactions in people. In the Dynamic Conflict Model, these triggers are called hot buttons. The specific hot buttons that are measured are described in Chapter Two. You may already have identified some of your own hot buttons. They differ considerably from person to person. This may relate to Ekman's model that suggests some of the differences in emotional auto-appraisers are learned through individual life experiences, whatever their original source. It is clear that hot buttons hold an emotional charge. When they are pushed, it is quite likely that the person will attribute negative motives to the other person and become angry with that person, perhaps in ways that will lead him or her to overreact and set off the retaliatory cycle.

There are ways to handle these difficult triggers, and in some ways the processes are familiar. Although our buttons are being pushed by someone else's behaviors, it is unlikely we will be able to get him or her to change, although it may be worthwhile to try. The real key to cooling hot buttons is to look inside ourselves.

We need to reflect on why our own hot buttons are hot. What about these behaviors in others causes us to get so irritated? If, for example, you have a hot button related to abrasive behavior, you would get especially irritated with people who are sarcastic, arrogant, and insensitive to others. A first step to understanding this hot button would be to look at what about these kinds of behaviors makes you angry. You may get upset by an assault on your own sense of self-worth or by the injustice associated with an abrasive person who is putting down weaker people. Think about situations when your hot buttons have been pushed, and consider what aspects of the other person's behavior irritated you and why. We do not usually take time for such introspection, but it is exactly what is needed to begin to gain self-control of our hot buttons.

Gene had a particularly sensitive hot button: he became annoyed with people who were untrustworthy. He felt that when someone makes a promise, it is a matter of honor to live up to it. People who treated promises in a cavalier manner really bothered him—so much so that he would show his anger and demean them in public. In working with Gene, the key question became how to confront untrustworthy people in a way that held them accountable but did not cause Gene to lose his cool, as well as respect from others. The first steps were to learn how to temper his emotional reaction to the behaviors of others so that he kept from getting off balance. He explored the reasons that untrustworthy behavior bothered him so much and considered how he wanted to respond when dealing with people acting in that manner. He also planned how to delay his initial responses in case he started to get angry. This would let him regain his balance and take time to think of alternative explanations for the behaviors (Capobianco, Davis, and Kraus, 2004). Gene followed this up by using constructive techniques of holding others accountable when they were untrustworthy (Patterson, Grenny, McMillan, and Switzler, 2005).

Hot buttons are closely associated with attribution. When someone pushes our hot buttons, it is very easy to attribute a bad motive as the cause of this action. Since our thoughts about others' motives are often based on speculation and they are so often wrong, we need to explore alternative explanations for the other person's actions. For example, in the case of an abrasive boss, it would be easy to associate arrogant behavior with an oversized ego. It could just as well be caused by an inferiority complex that the boss is trying to cover up by putting others down.

Exploring alternative motivations will not necessarily make the other person's behavior more pleasant or even acceptable, but it may change our own reaction to it. Get in the habit of asking yourself whether there could be multiple reasons that the other person is acting in a particular way. By doing this rather than being thrown off balance by the strong emotions that arise when your hot buttons are pushed, you can have more control over them and will be less likely to overreact in ways that you might later regret.

Hot buttons and the emotions associated with them can come on very quickly. It will not always be easy to keep from reacting to their heat, but conflict competent leaders will work to decrease the likelihood of their causing unfavorable reactions. Cooling hot buttons may take time and effort, but the resulting increase in self-control will be worth it.

Ekman (2003) suggests we need to develop a type of emotional consciousness that involves being more attentive to our own emotions as they are happening. If you become angry at someone, it is relatively easy for that anger to cause you to lash out almost without thinking. If instead you can be more aware of your own anger as it arises, it becomes easier to make a conscious choice of whether to respond. If you start to feel as if you are being thrown off balance by strong emotions, it is best to stop and try to regain balance. A variety of relaxation and breathing techniques can be employed to help cool down, as can centering techniques employed in the martial arts (Capobianco, Davis, and Kraus, 2004; Crum, 1987). Our balance can be restored before we take steps that may inadvertently provoke the other person.

Managing Behaviors

In the last stage of the retaliatory cycle, emotions are aroused either through hot buttons being pushed or from some other processes. At that point, we face the choice of how to respond. The Dynamic Conflict Model suggests that at this point, the choice is to use constructive or destructive responses. The destructive behaviors are fight-or-flight responses that tend to enflame and prolong conflict, largely by provoking destructive responses in the other person that escalate the retaliatory cycle. People often default to these survival types of responses even though they are counterproductive in modern organizational contexts. In contrast, constructive responses can be used to lessen tensions and lead conflict toward productive resolutions. We will explore these destructive and constructive responses to conflict in Chapters Four and Five. One constructive behavior that is particularly helpful in emotional contexts is Delay Responding, which slows things down and gives us time to let anger or other emotions dissipate before responding.

Conflict is all about emotions, and conflict competent leaders are emotionally intelligent. They know when their emotions are rising and are attentive when dealing with people whose behaviors might trigger their hot buttons. They are wary of speculating about the motives of others and use constructive behaviors to slow responses when emotions are running high and later work to determine what is really behind the other person's actions. These skills take time to develop. Building self-awareness is a first step. This is followed by practice. Sometimes this can take place in training and coaching contexts. In most cases, it needs to be used in real-life contexts. Mistakes will be made. They always do whenever we are learning new skills. Fortunately, we do not have to become experts. If others sense we are trying, they will be willing to give us the benefit of the doubt. A better environment will begin to emerge, and we will be on the way to improved conflict competence.

4

PREVENTING DESTRUCTIVE RESPONSES TO CONFLICT

> Mankind must evolve for all human conflict a
> method which rejects revenge, aggression, and
> retaliation. The foundation of such a method is
> love.
>
> —*Martin Luther King Jr.*

The speed with which the world today demands that leaders communicate, resolve problems, and make decisions interferes with their ability to effectively and carefully examine conflicts when they occur. Leaders are expected to spot opportunities and problems quickly, act on them immediately, and show results instantly. But when those opportunities and problems are conflict related, speed is not necessarily a virtue. Indeed, much of what we have learned about conflict competent leaders demonstrates that the most effective approaches to conflict seem to require careful and thoughtful understanding. Speed sometimes causes leaders to misidentify conflicts as ordinary problems or opportunities. Rapid solutions or responses therefore can miss the mark. Conflict competence requires understanding what behaviors and approaches can cause conflict to continue or, worse, escalate. It also includes the ability to discern conflict and comprehend its intensity. In this chapter, we discuss how conflict looks as it intensifies and examine the behaviors that hinder successful resolution of conflict.

Murphy's Law warns, paraphrased a bit, "If it can go wrong, it will go wrong." With conflict, there is plenty that can go wrong. When two people have different views, the potential exists for a plethora of problems. By studying what can go wrong during conflict, leaders are able to understand many of the factors that can result in seemingly insurmountable issues and irresolvable situations.

One way to begin is to consider the intensity levels associated with conflicts. Much like the scales meteorologists use to measure the intensity levels of hurricanes, cyclones, and tornadoes, there is a progression of intensity as a conflict evolves. The intensity of a hurricane, for instance, directly relates to the amount of damage forecasters expect when the storm makes landfall. A Category One storm is described as one with lower winds, and predictions are for minimal damage. Citizens and agencies make preparations accordingly. A Category Five storm is the most destructive type. Winds and rainfall will be of maximum intensity and can produce catastrophic damage. Citizens in the most exposed areas take steps to secure their property and ensure their safety during the storm.

The similarities between conflict and severe storms are useful in clarifying the notions of intensity and preparation. At the same time, there are major differences worth noting. It is impossible for anyone to change the course of the storm in ways that change its intensity or path. People can only prepare, endure, and recover. In contrast, interpersonal conflicts can be drastically influenced in ways that fundamentally change their intensity and path. It is this characteristic of conflict that makes our study of it so passionate and optimistic. Personal choices can make a difference. Leaders can alter the course of potentially damaging interactions by changing their approaches and responses when conflicts occur. Actions before, during, and after conflict are not limited to weathering the storm. On the contrary, individual actions can literally transform the climate. Individuals are active participants in establishing their own weather. Unlike the predicament when preparing for severe weather, leaders are not at the mercy of the elements during conflict.

Intensity Levels

Recalling our definition of *conflict*—"any situation in which people have apparently incompatible interests, goals, principles, or feelings"—we see that intensity begins at very low levels. In fact, in the earliest stages of conflict, most people may not perceive any intensity. As conflict evolves, however, the intensity may grow to painful proportions. We suggest the following intensity levels related to conflict situations:

Level One: Differences
Level Two: Misunderstandings
Level Three: Disagreements
Level Four: Discord
Level Five: Polarization

Level One: Differences

A few years ago, the Tampa Bay Buccaneers played the Oakland Raiders in the Super Bowl. As a resident of the Tampa Bay area, I (Tim) was caught up in the excitement of having my home team play for the world title. I had followed the team throughout the season and was convinced this was a team of destiny. My brother-in-law Harry, a lifelong Oakland Raiders fan, saw things differently. His beloved black-and-silver-clad warriors had celebrated championships in the past and were on a playoff roll. Harry was equally convinced that the Raiders were destined to win it all. During good-natured phone calls leading up to the game, we traded rationales for our beliefs and listed the virtues of our teams. Neither of us is an expert on football. We are "informed fans," and we love to watch the game, especially when our favorite team is playing. Obviously we saw it differently, and our differences were clear. (Note to Harry: the Bucs won!)

This is a good example of Intensity Level One, or Differences. Harry and I obviously had very different views about the game. We both could articulate reasons for our views and back up our views with sound arguments. We understood the other's views and positions very well. And although we both had passion for our positions, there really wasn't any heat in the disagreement. In other words, there was no discernable intensity to our disagreement. As it relates to our intensity scale, the definition of Differences is *when two people see a situation differently, understand the other party's position and interests well, and feel no discomfort regarding the difference.*

A conflict at this level of intensity seldom escalates into anything damaging. That's the good news. But occasionally escalation does occur. Let's take a look at how one of the football conversations might have escalated beyond Differences into something more intense:

Harry: The Bucs have been the laughingstock of professional football for years. What makes you think they can handle the pressure of a championship game?

Tim: The past is the past. That has nothing to do with the team today. They've done everything one could ask. They're gaining confidence every week.

Harry: Well, that's the whole deal with pressure. Everything matters. No one can prepare for the kind of pressure associated with a game like this unless they've been there before. My team has been there.

Tim: Your team? Your team? When did they become *your* team? I mean, you don't even live in the same state. They're in California and you're in Ohio. What kind of a fan is that?

Harry: Hey, c'mon. I've been a fan for as long as I can remember. Proximity doesn't make fans. Passion does. And besides, you haven't always been a Bucs fan. How long did it take you to get on board with them after growing up in Ohio? You're a "jump on the bandwagon" kind of fan.

Tim: Take a hike, buddy. At least I pull for my home town team. Not some team a couple of thousand miles away.

Harry: Yeah? At least I don't jump from one team to another. I have loyalty, man.

Tim: Don't give me that. You just can't admit that you're a lousy fan.

Thankfully, this conversation never happened, but it could have. For the sake of argument and to make a point, let's pretend it did. At the moment when the conversation began to be person focused instead of issue focused, the intensity level turned up a notch. Neither party was prepared for the increase in intensity. Neither probably remembers how it happened. It may be difficult, even impossible, for them to pinpoint the exact moment the intensity increased. But both could sense the difference in the communication. It is possible that both Harry and Tim might blame the other for a comment that led to the escalation, or they might blame themselves. It is likely that both regret that the intensity got a bit higher than they intended. Now they have a degree of conflict that requires attention. Understanding that even a Difference, a conflict with no current discomfort, can progress quickly up the intensity scale is important in becoming a conflict competent leader.

Remembering that one of our key premises is that conflict is welcome and even desirable in the workplace, it's critical not to be lulled to sleep by the friendly differences we encounter regularly. At the same time, there's no need to become paranoid about the differences we encounter daily. There is, though, a fine line separating a friendly difference of opinion and the beginning of a potentially damaging disagreement than one may at first perceive. The risk and reward nature of conflict must be regarded with respect. Embracing differences is almost always beneficial. Allowing differences to be catalysts for harm is one of the most frequent causes of conflict becoming destructive.

Level Two: Misunderstandings

Dennis was one of the most reliable team members ever in the maintenance department. He was never late with an assignment, always completed projects on time and with excellent results, and could be counted on to step up whenever circumstances called for extra effort. His boss, Jim, considered himself and the organization lucky that Dennis had eschewed opportunities elsewhere. Dennis was clearly a model employee. It was this characterization that made the current situation so much more confusing. Dennis was late for the most important staff meeting of the year, and Jim was growing more concerned by the minute. "What in the world can Dennis be thinking?" wondered Jim. Little did Jim know that Dennis was busy at work in another part of the building, concerned only about his current task.

The week before, Jim and Dennis had spoken about the importance of the next meeting. Dennis was flattered that Jim had asked him to make a brief presentation when members of the executive board would be in attendance. It was not often that someone at Dennis's level was asked to attend, let alone present, during a meeting of this importance. Typically the staff meetings, which were held every other month, involved only members of the immediate team and sometimes Jim's boss. Jim told Dennis how confident he was in his abilities and said he was sure Dennis "would do a bang-up job presenting." Jim emphasized that the meeting was more structured than usual and that timeliness and sticking to the agenda were critical. He said the meeting was set for Tuesday, the 11th, at 10:00 A.M. He also told Dennis he would send him a reminder e-mail.

Sure enough, the next day Dennis received the e-mail. The text read, "The meeting begins promptly at 10:00 A.M. on Tuesday, the 11th . . ." It continued, "I'm really looking forward to your presentation. I know the board members are too."

So where did the communication break down? How could two well-meaning people not be on the same wavelength for a meeting of such importance? Maybe most important, how was it possible that Jim's expectation and Dennis's expectation were so vastly different that Dennis was clueless about the problem? The simplicity of the answer will not be surprising to many of you who have experienced similar circumstances. We sometimes call it the "danger of cruise control." Others call it "making assumptions." Most of us call it a misunderstanding.

Jim and Dennis were very clear and in agreement about the bulk of the situation. It was a critical meeting. Dennis would be presenting to a high-level audience. Jim was confident in his ability. The meeting was to begin at 10:00 A.M. on Tuesday the 11th. So there Jim was waiting for Dennis to appear by 10:00 A.M. on that Tuesday, February 11. And there Dennis was going about his business elsewhere while Jim simmered in disbelief. Dennis thought the meeting was Tuesday, *March* 11, the date of the next normally scheduled meeting. Neither had been clear about the month of the meeting; both assumed it was clear to the other. The clarity of all the other facts in the situation led both to believe that they had a common understanding, and the long history of mutual respect and familiarity between Jim and Dennis created a comfortable atmosphere. This combination sets the stage for miscommunication due to cruise control, a situation when it is easy to make the assumption that everything is understood. This is how a simple misunderstanding can become a potentially serious conflict.

Regarding the intensity scale, we define Misunderstandings as *times or situations where what is understood by one party is different from what is understood by the other party.* The reason for the misunderstanding is key to resolving the issue, but is not important as it relates to the intensity of the conflict. What is important is that the parties recognize the misunderstanding and address it rather than allow it to evolve into a more damaging level of conflict. A misunderstanding in and of itself does not create a great degree of intensity. But the longer a misunderstanding lingers, the more intensity it can generate. The more important the issue that is misunderstood, the higher the potential is for increased escalation of intensity. For these reasons, conflict competent leaders must take steps to increase the likelihood of shared understanding in all communications. When misunderstandings occur (and they will), they must address the misunderstanding for what it is and not succumb to "intention invention" or "accelerated assumptions," both of which can lead to escalation of the conflict.

In the case of Jim and Dennis, a good outcome of the misunderstanding would have been a conversation something like this:

Jim: Dennis, I was very upset when you didn't show up at the meeting on time. Actually I was pretty much beside myself.

Dennis: I'll bet you were. I know how important this meeting was. I'm glad you found me, and we were able to recover, even though I had to wing my presentation.

Jim: Yeah, it was better than your missing the entire meeting, that's for sure. I want to figure out why we weren't on top of this, though. How did this happen?

Dennis: I'm sorry for the inconvenience and for putting you on the spot. You know I'd never do that on purpose. I think I just assumed the meeting was at our regularly scheduled time next month.

Jim: And I assumed that because it was a special meeting, you understood it was out of the ordinary in terms of the date. I thought sure I said the meeting was next week.

Dennis: You were clear that it was special and important. You even reiterated it in your e-mail. But even the e-mail didn't say anything about next week or February. I probably should have asked for clarification, though, because it was so important.

Jim: Well, I should have been clearer about the meeting taking place this week. It's a shame that something so simple became such a problem.

Dennis: Yes. I won't take anything for granted next time. I'm glad we cleared up where the breakdown occurred.

Jim: Me too. Thanks for talking about it. Let's get back to work.

When conflicts due to misunderstandings take place, the potential is great for the intensity of the conflict to escalate rapidly. Therefore, it's imperative that the parties check for misunderstandings early in the process. The earlier a misunderstanding is identified, the less intensity it will generate. In addition, once a misunderstanding is discovered, conflict competent leaders focus on the correction necessary to clear up the misunderstanding rather than dwell on the confusing circumstances. Finally, conflict competent leaders take steps in all their communications to limit the opportunities for misunderstandings. As we'll discuss at more length in the next chapter, checking for understanding and perspective taking are key skills for this purpose.

Level Three: Disagreements

Disagreements are basically Differences with an attitude. Our definition of Disagreement is *when two people see a situation differently and, regardless of how well they understand the other's position and interests, feel discomfort that the other party disagrees.* The key factor in a disagreement, as related to the intensity scale, is the degree of discomfort that one or both parties experience. Disagreements are not inherently negative. They may actually be necessary for discovering the underlying differences that can be crucial to new ideas, change, solutions to problems, and creativity. A Disagreement may signal the need to slow down and examine the communication for unaligned perspectives that can just as easily drive innovation as conflict. The reason Disagreements are considered Level Three in intensity is their potential for leading to damage.

Most of us can easily recall Disagreements at work, at home, and in a variety of social settings. It is reasonable to believe that most do little damage or are resolved with relative ease. We'd venture to say that many are rather quickly forgotten or dismissed as long as no pattern of Disagreement is evident with the same conflict partner. The danger with Disagreements lies in two specific areas. First, the potential for a Disagreement to escalate is much greater than a Difference and at least equal to Misunderstanding. There is a degree of emotion involved, which is often the fuel for generating the heat in conflicts. Second, because we are all programmed to spot trends and patterns, we are quite adept at spotting any series of Disagreements with the same person. Once people see a trend of Disagreements, they are more likely to slip into blaming, labeling, attributing, and otherwise making assumptions about the other person. Obviously such reasoning enables conflict to evolve to more destructive levels.

Jeanne is an elementary school guidance counselor, and Harriet is the principal of the school. In today's turbulent society, there are a myriad of issues surrounding the health and well-being of young students. School administrators and teachers are often in positions to spot potential cases of abuse or neglect. One such unfortunate circumstance provided the basis of a disagreement between Jeanne and Harriet. Here's how the discussion unfolded:

Jeanne: I sent you a report yesterday regarding the situation with Kevin G. I expected you to get back to me before the end of school.

Harriet: Yes. I reviewed your report. The injuries you described do concern me. But these injuries could have been the result of any number of situations that aren't abuse related.

Jeanne: But we are required to report suspicious injuries, especially when the child indicates that the injuries were caused by an adult. When I didn't hear from you, I was very concerned that we hadn't taken any steps to protect this child.

Harriet: Our duty is to report clear cases of abuse. And our duty is to provide a safe environment in which our students can learn. Our duty isn't to make accusations.

Jeanne: This has nothing to do with accusations. None of us is entirely comfortable reporting potential abuse because it may turn out to be explainable and the parent or guardian might be upset. But that's certainly better than putting a student, a child, at risk of physical harm. I thought we had a policy that required us to report these things. Why didn't you follow up?

Harriet: In my judgment, what you reported didn't warrant follow-up. I have to make tough decisions every day. The injuries you reported didn't meet the test for concluding that abuse was evident.

Jeanne: I disagree. And there's no test for it! You didn't see the child. You didn't see the injuries. I followed our procedure for reporting and expected that we would take steps to protect this student.

Harriet: You did follow our procedures: you sent a report to me. I also followed procedures and decided against taking additional steps or filing a report with Child Services. We'll keep your report on file, and if there are other incidents, we'll be able to compare the situations. That's procedure.

Jeanne: I'm washing my hands of this. I do not want to be responsible if something bad happens to him. You're the principal.
I know it's your call. I just don't agree.

Harriet: You don't have to agree. You followed our procedures. So
you did your job. I appreciate that.

Jeanne: Funny. I don't feel very appreciated.

The Disagreement between Harriet and Jeanne has many emotional entanglements. The fact that a child is at the center of their
disagreement certainly tugs at our heartstrings. The very notion of
child abuse is nauseating. Harriet and Jeanne have no disagreement
about that. What is instructive about this situation is the degree of
discomfort Harriet and Jeanne feel about their Disagreement. Harriet acknowledges Jeanne's position and even acknowledges her ad-
herence to procedure. Jeanne acknowledges Harriet's role and her
power to make decisions. What goes unaddressed are the feelings,
the discomfort, associated with their Disagreement. It is this factor
that distinguishes a Disagreement from a Difference.

One final thought about Disagreements: when we hear that two
people have "agreed to disagree," we usually cringe just a little bit
on the inside. In reality, when parties proclaim they have "agreed
to disagree," they have at best agreed that their differences are not
severe and the consequences of their differences are very mild. In
some cases, the parties may in fact be describing a Difference rather
than a Disagreement. We fear, though, that "the agreement to disagree" is loaded with hidden booby traps. It is quite likely that emotions have been ignored and the situation is bound to rear its ugly
head again in the near future. Emotions unaddressed and left to fester will undoubtedly lead to a continuation of the Disagreement or
worse: an escalation to a higher level of intensity. Our advice is that
when you "agree to disagree," use that very statement as a signal to
proceed with caution. Continue talking with your conflict partner
about your agreement with the intent of reaching a new agreement
that you see the situation differently. Talk openly and honestly
about your emotions. As emotions are acknowledged and discussed,
chances are the intensity level is substantially decreased.

Level Four: Discord

When a conflict reaches the level of Discord, it is characterized by a generally deteriorating relationship between the conflict partners. The discomfort they feel is apparent not only when addressing the conflict issue but during most, if not all, of their interactions. The relationship suffers because of the intensity of the conflict. Our definition of Discord is *situations where the conflict causes difficulties in the relationship of the people involved even when they are not dealing with the original conflict.*

How many of us have found ourselves behaving poorly with someone with whom we work because we've had a recent conflict that's unresolved? See if you can recall a time when you have behaved in any of the following ways:

- Averted your eyes to avoid direct eye contact with another person in a meeting
- Turned your back when you noticed a recent conflict partner approaching you in a public area
- Pretended to be engaged in a conversation with someone else (perhaps even faking a telephone call) to avoid interacting with a conflict partner
- Declined an invitation to a social event because you suspected the other person would be in attendance
- Found an excuse to miss a meeting that your conflict partner would attend
- Criticized an idea or suggestion made by a conflict partner even though the idea or suggestion was reasonable
- Refused to support a proposal made by the other person based not on the merits of the proposal but because it was simply his or her idea
- Given up on an idea or position quickly when challenged by your conflict partner just to avoid any more conflict
- Used sarcasm or laughed at an idea proposed by the other person

- Continued to push one of your own ideas in a meeting well after it has become apparent that your conflict partner's idea is better

It's tempting to say, "If you answered yes to three or more of these questions, then you are at risk for CIBBS [conflict-induced bad behavior syndrome], and you should seek immediate medical attention." Of course, as far as we know, CIBBS is not actually a medical condition. And to be entirely truthful, we just made up the acronym. Nevertheless, each of the ten examples is an actual behavior we have observed or that has been reported to us by those experiencing conflict. And as we will explore later, each of these behaviors fits the description of a destructive behavior.

The point is that once a conflict reaches the level of Discord, the parties involved begin to experience ongoing difficulties with their relationship. When a person begins to respond to a conflict partner by avoiding, criticizing, yielding, demeaning, blocking, scheming, or sabotaging, (you get the picture), it is clear that the relationship is suffering and both parties are experiencing discomfort. Serious damage to the relationship can result if the conflict is not addressed effectively.

Level Five: Polarization

When the parties in a conflict begin "recruiting" others to join their cause, it is a sure sign of Polarization. Another defining characteristic is associated with the sheer volume of effort one or both parties puts into defending his or her position or making his or her case. A third clue of Polarization is the refusal to engage in constructive behaviors such as Perspective Taking, Creating Solutions, Expressing Emotions, or Reaching Out. (Constructive behaviors are discussed in more detail in Chapter Five.) The most common outcomes of Polarization are that the conflict goes unresolved and the relationship of the conflict participants deteriorates. In the most severe stages of Polarization, the parties actively use destructive behaviors with one another, including Demeaning Others, Displaying

Anger, and Retaliating. Such actions signal the most intense level of conflict. If the two people involved were countries, one would describe the situation as being on the brink of war. Our definition of Polarization is *conflict situations characterized by severe negative emotions and behavior with little or no hope for reconciliation*.

In our discussions with those who have found themselves at this most intense level of conflict, two common themes seem to be present. One is the apparent inability or unwillingness of the conflict partners to try to see the other party's side of the story. The differences between the parties are so severe that accusations and attributions become common. Working toward some sort of resolution seems completely futile. The second theme is the active recruitment of others to support one's position.

Consider the case of two coworkers whose conflict evolved to this level. James and Renee are sales team leaders for a pharmaceuticals company. Sales teams are recognized for the volume of sales calls made each month and rewarded with a lavish dinner. More important, the sales team with the most calls each month had "bragging rights" and the competition was always spirited. During a recent meeting, new guidelines for tracking and counting sales calls were instituted. James thought the new guidelines were unfair and intended to handicap his team because they had been leading the company in sales calls every month for the past year. He knew that Renee's region had been number two for most of this period and made no effort to hide his enthusiasm at beating her month after month. He also knew that Renee had been lobbying for new guidelines that would potentially tilt the outcome her team's way.

Over the past few months, their relationship had become more and more antagonistic. During meetings when new guidelines were discussed, they could barely hide their disdain for one another. Steely glares across the table were commonplace, and words were often exchanged. The real fireworks, though, often occurred after the meetings. In the hallway outside the conference room after one meeting, James loudly accused Renee of "being so competitive that she stacked the deck when playing gin rummy with her kids."

Renee retorted, "Your problem isn't so much that you can't stand to lose; it's that you can't see that you're a loser." Luckily, cooler heads prevailed, and James and Renee were ushered to distant areas of the office. As is the case in Polarization, the parties went their separate ways, but nothing was resolved. Neither party could see the other's point of view or was willing even to consider an alternative.

As suggested earlier, another common theme of Polarization is recruitment. The conflict partners are so entrenched in their own position and so convinced of the rightness of their view that they often begin to recruit others to be "on their side." In the case of Renee and James, the conversations after the hallway confrontation are prime examples. Just minutes after the hallway altercation, James moved from openly bashing Renee to trying to convince his colleagues to support his position over hers. "Look," he said, "I don't know what her problem is, but I can tell you that changing the guidelines is bad for all of us. You all know that I love being number one, but that's not the point. The point is that we've trained our people to succeed based on a tried-and-true formula. Now she wants to change all that because of a stupid monthly contest. How can anyone support a change for that kind of reasoning? The old system has worked for years. Don't you agree?" If successful, James will convince some of his colleagues to take his side. Renee may do the same. And the conflict that originated between two parties may expand to include multiple parties and levels of complexity that can have a detrimental impact on the organization for years.

Summary

The intensity levels of conflict are important to consider for several reasons. First, a conflict competent leader must be able to recognize conflict. The more intense conflicts are easier to spot but are also potentially more complex. A leader who spots only conflicts that are at the higher intensity levels may find that these conflicts are more difficult to handle and may have an impact on more people than originally thought.

Second, the earlier that conflicts are detected, the more willing the parties are to explore their differences. As we suggest throughout this book, conflict should be embraced as an opportunity to examine diverse thoughts, ideas, and creative solutions. The earlier the conflict is detected or when the conflict is at a lower level of intensity, the more embraceable it may be. In other words, when conflict appears as a Difference, a Misunderstanding, or a Disagreement, the heat or emotion in the conflict is less intense. The conflict may be more approachable at these levels not just as a function of how resolvable it is, but how useful it may be.

Finally, understanding the intensity levels can be helpful to leaders in assessing their own responses to conflict situations. As leaders encounter conflict in the organization, they will find themselves involved in some of them as participants. Knowing the signs of intensity can assist them in monitoring their own responses and reactions so they can choose to cool, or deintensify, the conflict through their words and actions.

Destructive Behaviors

One problem with conflict is that so many people respond to it poorly. Conflict itself is not the problem. On the contrary, conflict is really pretty special, even intriguing. One of our favorite energizers in our seminars and training programs is to project an unclear image on the screen for a few moments, remove it, and then ask the audience to describe what they saw. One of the all-time classics is the line drawing that seen one way resembles an elderly woman and seen another resembles a much younger woman. Those in the audience who see the image of the elderly woman confidently describe the older lady with details of her scarf, weathered skin, slight build, and tired gaze into the distance on the left. Hardly able to contain themselves, those who see the younger woman rattle off their descriptions: the fancy feathered hat, long formal dress, spiffy jacket, and confident focus of the young woman toward the back right of the screen. When pressed for more details, both sides provide only a few but are absolutely convinced of the rightness of their view. We ask the class for a breakdown by show of hands of who sees which woman. Then we prepare to show the image a second time and instruct the class members to look for the "other" image this time. Shortly after projecting the image, amid chuckles and "Oh my goshes," everyone in the classroom can see the other image, and they can easily go back and forth between the images in their mind's eye. It's fascinating and fun, amusing and engaging. Some would even say intriguing. And nobody is the least bit offended, hurt, or damaged by the conflict. So why don't we respond to every conflict with fascination, amusement, engagement, and intrigue? Why indeed. Therein lies the wonder and the motivation for leaders to harness the extraordinary potential of conflict.

People Behaving Poorly: Reactions and Reflexes

So much has been researched and written about people's responses to conflict. With apologies to those who study the science of behavior, one thing seems extraordinarily clear to us: there are some responses to conflict that individuals choose, and there are others that they do not choose. It is important that the conflict competent leader understand both.

First, there are the hard-wired responses to conflict. Through genetic evolution, human beings come equipped to respond to conflict situations in some very predictable ways. For instance, when confronted with a situation that causes fear or anger, the adrenal glands pump adrenaline into the bloodstream, causing bodies to go on high alert. People don't choose to have their glands respond this way; they just do. And then they have to deal with the consequences. Similarly, there's a point in conflict where one's body defaults to fight-or-flight responses, causing the same kind of adrenaline rush. People don't choose this; their bodies just react.

Then the brains get into the act. Again, oversimplifying this to its most elementary level, the brain begins to divert blood flow based on what it considers the current highest-priority functions:

running away or doing battle. So more blood is pumped toward the muscles in the legs, arms, torso, and back and *away* from the brain. Arguably, at the time of most need, people's bodies are programmed to handicap their center of reasoning while energizing their abilities for fight or flight.

Armed with the knowledge that all human beings have similar fight-or-flight responses to conflict-related situations, the conflict competent leader is better prepared for the earliest reactions to conflict. The leader understands what a colleague means when he or she says, "I don't know what I was thinking when I snapped at Pete like that." Essentially everyone has the same biological factory equipment for responding to conflict. And there are times when that equipment kicks in and people react. The conflict competent leader knows this. The conflict competent leader also knows that human beings have additional factory equipment that enables them to reason and choose. The reflexes and reactions that served our ancient ancestors well in times of danger are almost always ineffective for handling conflicts today. With some effort, nearly everyone can override the early fight-or-flight reactions and select better responses.

Much of this chapter is devoted to describing behaviors that may emanate from the depths of our biological hard wiring but are poor choices for engaging in effective conflict interactions. The better everyone, including leaders, understands these poor choices or destructive behaviors, the better able they are to choose more effective responses that enable resolution, satisfaction, and progress.

People Behaving Poorly: Choices and Tactics

As we discussed earlier in this book, Dan Dana, in his book, *Managing Differences* (2005), speaks eloquently about the phenomenon he calls the "retaliatory cycle." He suggests that most arguments have a common anatomy: a triggering event, the perception of threat, defensive anger, acting out, and repetition. A triggering event is any behavior by a person that may or may not be intended as hostile but is perceived as threatening by another person. This perception of threat is accompanied by a natural emotional response to the perceived threat he calls defensive anger. The acting-out phase is critical. It is here that the person feeling threatened behaves in ways that either cause the conflict to escalate through retaliation, anger, or violence or solidify the conflict through distancing, avoiding, or yielding. These behaviors may be simple reactions that occur without much thought. More likely, even though they may be emotionally charged, the behaviors are selected or chosen to provide an intended result: self-protection. Such behaviors are in turn perceived by the first person as threatening, and the cycle repeats endlessly. Conflict competence includes the ability to identify and understand the destructive responses that fuel the retaliatory cycle. Leaders who can do this effectively are in a position to spot conflicts early and decide how best to deal with them in constructive ways.

How people respond to conflict situations spans a lengthy continuum from fight to flight. Each situation is different, and people's responses, both cognitive and emotional, may differ accordingly. In one situation, they may find themselves withdrawing from the situation as quickly and completely as possible. In another, they may seethe with anger and prepare to defend their positions at all costs. The conflict competent leader must grapple with this continuum on multiple levels. First, the leader must be able to self-diagnose and have a high degree of self-awareness in order to handle personal conflicts effectively. This is critical not only for practical purposes, but to model effective behaviors and establish credibility in the organization. Second, the leader must be an expert observer of others so evidence of conflict can be spotted early. Third, the leader must be able and willing to intervene, coach, and influence those in conflict. Understanding the range of ineffective responses is crucial to the leader's ability in these areas. Finally, the conflict competent leader's ultimate task is to build organizational competence. At this level, members of the organization are self-monitoring, and the leader must view the range of conflict behaviors from a strategic point of view.

We believe most of the destructive responses to conflict are based on choice. Everyone can think of those times when they "just snapped," "spoke without thinking," "reacted impulsively," or otherwise remember the bad behavior as if victimized by some strange, uncontrollable power. By and large, though, everyone has the very controllable power of choice. And if they are really honest with themselves, during conflict many resort to tactics and behaviors designed to cause discomfort, delay progress, disrupt communication, or even inflict pain. Conflict competent leaders more often choose constructive responses to conflict while rejecting destructive responses, and they help those around them do the same. Examining and understanding these destructive behaviors is a critical step in becoming conflict competent.

In 1999, our colleagues Sal Capobianco, Mark Davis, and Linda Kraus published the Conflict Dynamics Profile, a groundbreaking 360-degree assessment instrument focused entirely on conflict behaviors. We rely heavily on their work as we describe the choices people make during conflict that escalate the conflict or contribute to continuing discord and polarization. They identified two sets of Destructive Behaviors: Active and Passive. We'll focus on the Active Destructive Behaviors here and address Passive Destructive Behaviors later in the chapter.

Active Destructive Behaviors.   Active Destructive Behaviors are those in which the individual overtly responds to a conflict situation. These require some effort and almost always escalate the conflict. One way to differentiate between Active and Passive behaviors is to think of Active Behaviors as doing or saying something, while Passive Behaviors are characterized by withholding or refraining. Active Destructive Behaviors are typically among the most toxic responses one can have in working relationships.

Winning at All Costs.   An individual who absolutely refuses to budge from a position, steadfastly sticks to a "my way or the highway" strategy, or continues to vehemently argue for his or her way well after a different course of action has been taken is exhibiting the signs of Winning at All Costs.

Perseverance is a virtue. Tenacity is a heralded leadership trait. Decisiveness is critical in today's business environment. And to quote Vince Lombardi, legendary head coach of the Green Bay Packers when they were a dynasty in the National Football League during the 1960s, "Winning isn't the main thing, it's the only thing." So what's wrong with a Winning at All Costs attitude? In many situations, it is exactly what's needed. Would you want your heart surgeon to feel any other way when it comes to your or your loved one's open heart surgery? Would you like your home town baseball team to enter Game 7 of the World Series thinking "there's always next year"? Would you prefer actor Bill Pullman, playing the role of president of the United States in the blockbuster film *Independence Day*, to declare in the face of total annihilation by aliens, "I guess we'll just go quietly into the night"? Of course not. When it comes to interpersonal conflict, though, extreme tenacity and perseverance can be easily interpreted as counterproductive or hostile.

An example of Winning at All Costs behavior is illustrated by an incident experienced by James and Renee, the two combative pharmaceutical sales team leaders we mentioned earlier. The regional sales office is equipped with two teleconferencing rooms. One is small and designed for just one or two participants, while the other is large and can accommodate a group. James had previously reserved the large, more desirable room for a call with his field team. Renee had a promising lead develop and wanted to bring in several staff members for a call to a potential new client. She approached James about switching teleconference rooms:

Renee: James, would you mind trading conference rooms today?
James: Why would I want to do that?
Renee: Well, I have invited several others to participate in a call with a potential new client and wanted to use the larger room so we could fit comfortably. I thought you were just making a call to your field staff and wouldn't need the large room.

James: You thought wrong. I need the larger room.

Renee: But aren't you the only one on the call on this end?

James: I said no. I scheduled the room because I need it.

Renee: Okay. I noticed you have it reserved for the entire afternoon. You're just having your weekly call with field staff. Will you really need it for that entire time? Could I have it beginning at 3:00?

James: No (smiling).

Renee: How about I buy you lunch to switch?

James: Nope.

Renee: Come on, James. There's no real reason you need the large room. I really do.

James: I reserved it. I keep it.

Renee: You're just being obstinate. Why do you always have to be this way?

James: (still smiling) I'm just that good.

Renee: Fine. Have a nice call.

Frustrated by the encounter, Renee walks away thinking that James is acting like a spoiled brat who always has to have his way. She silently vows to remember this incident when he needs a favor, no matter how small. She'll show him.

The obvious consequences of James's Winning at All Costs behavior are that he gets to keep the large conference room, he has a feeling of satisfaction for winning the argument, and Renee is frustrated. The less obvious consequences are those that make this behavior so destructive. Although James is aware of Renee's frustration, he may not understand her resolve to retaliate in the future. He may perceive the entire episode as humorous rather than relationship damaging. For Renee, this is just one more incident in an already strained relationship. It further cements her commitment to "defeat" James in the future and find ways to interfere with his progress as he seems to do toward her so often. She also feels a little disenchanted that she and James can't find ways to get along. If they could get along, things would be so much better.

The basic premise of Winning at All Costs behavior is a win-lose outcome. Most people don't enjoy the prospect of losing. During a conflict, when one sees an advantage or a weakness in the other party's argument, it is tempting to seize it. After all, isn't success often associated with winning arguments? Another difficulty with Winning at All Costs is the sometimes less obvious impact of the behavior. As the interchange between James and Renee shows, the less obvious outcome of James's behavior is the deteriorating relationship with Renee, very likely leading to more damaging conflicts. In most interpersonal conflicts, the desired outcome is to resolve the conflict in a way that satisfies both or all parties, at least as much as possible. Winning at All Costs can take a terrible toll on working relationships and increase the likelihood of more conflict in the future.

Displaying Anger. During conflict when a person uses harsh language, yells, uses profanity, tries to intimidate the other party, or uses threatening gestures and facial expressions, the results are predictably negative. As a destructive behavioral category, Displaying Anger is perhaps the easiest to understand and interpret. It is classic "fight" (rather than flight) behavior. The potential results of Displaying Anger range from the other party's withdrawing or yielding to the other's behaving in kind. At either end of the spectrum, the result is an unresolved conflict and one that has likely escalated.

In our work with leaders, we find that displays of anger are thankfully infrequent when compared to the other categories of Destructive Behavior. The problem is that the behavior is so damaging that even sporadic displays cause severe difficulties in conflict resolution. It is easy to understand that such behavior is destructive. It is equally easy to identify the behavior when it occurs, especially if you're the offended party or an observer. (Sometimes, though, the person displaying anger is genuinely surprised that his or her conflict partner sees their behavior as so toxic. We have more to say on this phenomenon later.) What is not so easy is grasping the degree of damage that can be inflicted and the work it can take to heal the wounds. We have seen cases in which relationships still suffer even though years have passed since the original offending display of anger occurred.

We were working with a vice president from a large insurance company. Bob considered his working relationship with his boss, an executive vice president, to be "satisfying and enjoyable." We reviewed Bob's results on a multirater leadership assessment instrument and found the ratings of his boss to be very encouraging in most categories. His boss rated him at or above the median in every category except one dealing with sensitivity in interpersonal relationships. This did not come as a surprise to Bob; he knew his reputation for being demanding but fair. In a presession questionnaire, Bob had disclosed that earlier in his career, he had a tendency to lose his temper, but he had worked hard to overcome that issue. He was proud of his progress in this area. We also reviewed his results from the Conflict Dynamics Profile (Capobianco, Davis, and Kraus, 1999). Of great concern was his boss's assessment in the Displaying Anger category. His self-rating for Displaying Anger was in the mid- or average range, roughly at the fiftieth percentile for this category. His boss rated him in the "very high," or least favorable, range. In other words, the boss was indicating that Bob displayed anger in conflict situations to a degree that caused significant concern.

During the consultation with Bob, he continued to ponder with disbelief the perception of others, especially his boss. He said he was "shocked" that his boss saw him that way and couldn't imagine how he had formed that perception. He reiterated that he had worked diligently over the past few years to control the temper of his youth. We empathized and encouraged him to think of times he may have been perceived, even mistakenly so, by his boss or others to have displayed anger. We suggested that the intent of one's actions and behaviors may not always be understood by others. It would be worthwhile for him to put himself in others' shoes and try to see his behavior from their point of view. Finally, we suggested that Bob thank his boss for the feedback and inquire about the perception of his displays of anger. (This suggestion was not made lightly. We spent a considerable amount of time understanding Bob's relationship with his boss, coached him about his approach, and even role-played the conversation.)

During our next conversation with Bob, the reason for his boss's perception became clear. Bob rather excitedly described the talk he had had with his boss. There was good news and bad news. The good news was that his boss gave him plenty of credit for improving his temper and praised him for the efforts he made. The bad news was that his boss had still not completely forgiven Bob for an outburst that happened almost five years earlier. Apparently Bob had confronted his boss after a staff meeting and within earshot of others issued a profanity-laced accusation regarding his treatment during the meeting. Bob's boss replied that they would have to discuss it later and walked away. Later that evening, Bob apologized in a voice mail message. His boss replied, in a voice mail, to "forget it" and scheduled a time to discuss Bob's concern. Neither party remembers much about that next conversation or the resolution. But what the boss never forgot was the harsh, angry confrontation. He admitted that he had never really looked at Bob the same way since then and still harbored some bad feelings. And each time he observed Bob in heated situations, he always thought of that day in the hallway. In his mind, Bob was prone to display anger. Despite Bob's successful efforts to control his temper, the boss's perception was perpetually tarnished from that single costly interaction. Once damage is inflicted, the offended person's perception can be difficult to change. In this case, a single serious display of anger had had a significant impact for almost five years.

One other phenomenon sometimes associated with Displaying Anger is that the "displayer" sometimes doesn't realize the degree of pain he or she inflicts. In other words, the behavior hurts or looks worse to the receiver or observer than the person who exhibits the behavior. We have heard many offenders say things like, "Oh, it wasn't *that* bad," or, "They should know me well enough by now that I didn't mean it that way." This difference in perception can handicap a person's ability to accurately self-monitor or self-assess.

The best barometer for knowing whether one is displaying anger is in the eye of the beholder. Conflict situations are characterized by higher-than-normal stress and emotion, which often lead to magnification of intent. Our guidance is to rely on the observations of others when attempting to ascertain a person's level of Displaying Anger. For leaders, this is especially critical because the "magnification" mentioned above is multiplied even more with higher rank or level. When someone provides feedback that you looked or acted angrily during a conflict, we recommend you pay close attention. Determine what you said or did that caused the perception of anger. And work on those specific behaviors to improve the perception of others.

Demeaning Others. One of the most common forms of Demeaning Others is the perception of unfair criticism. When one party feels unfairly criticized, ridiculed, or singled out, the impact is almost always negative. Unfortunately, many incidents of Demeaning Others are unintended. Think of those times when you tried to provide some constructive criticism to a colleague, only to find your well-intended feedback rejected. Remember your attempts at humor to lighten a tense moment among coworkers, only to discover that your joke was taken literally and heightened the tension. Reflect on the times you actually said nothing at all to a conflict partner, but your body language or nonverbal actions sent a strong message. Regardless of intent, the effect of the behavior is often increased anger or hostility toward the sender and either an escalation of the conflict or a withdrawal from it. The impact is destructive, and resolution becomes more challenging.

For all the unintended expressions that result in the feeling of being demeaned, there are also times when the demeaning behavior is purposeful. Have you ever made a wisecrack at someone else's expense? Have you ever made openly critical comments about a colleague's work or efforts? Have you ever communicated negative vibes to someone in the form of looks, head movements, hand gestures, or posture? Or have you ever made those obnoxious auditory noises in the guise of a throat clear or sniff that demonstrate your disapproval or disdain? No one is perfect, and likely almost everyone has behaved in these ways at some point. But when people do, they are enflaming the situation and in some cases causing a conflict where none had previously existed. Let's examine the three major ways in which demeaning behavior occurs.

One form of demeaning behavior is associated with criticizing the actions or efforts of another person. The purpose of criticism is to provide information about one's expectations and standards. This is usually accomplished by comparing the actions, behaviors, or results perceived to the expectation or standard desired. When criticism is provided constructively, the receiver can welcome it. However, when it is uninvited or is perceived as unfair or harsh, the consequences can be quite severe.

Kathleen had made her first ever presentation to the executive team earlier in the day. She was relieved that it was over. Making formal presentations always caused her anxiety. Overall, she felt pretty good about her performance. During lunch, Pat, one of Kathleen's coworkers who had attended the meeting, asked if he could join Kathleen at her table. Kathleen recalled seeing Pat during the presentation but had not spoken with him since. Pat was the most experienced of her peers and had made many presentations to the executive team during his career. Kathleen had never worked closely with Pat, but knew of his reputation as a detail-oriented high achiever. She wondered if he would have anything to say about her presentation.

Pat: I'm glad I could attend your presentation today. I know this was your first time presenting to the executive team. I think I helped cover for you.

Kathleen: Thanks, I think. Yes, it was my first presentation to this group, and I was a little nervous. What do you mean you covered for me? I thought it went pretty well.

Pat: One thing I know the exec team expects from presenters is an outline of the main points. I noticed you didn't supply one.

Kathleen: That's right. I gave them a copy of my presentation slides instead.

Pat: Yes, but that is different. They like a single-page outline. It's standard.

Kathleen: Okay. That's good to know. I'll be sure to be prepared next time.

Pat: The last time someone didn't provide an outline, the team asked the presenter to postpone until they were prepared.

Kathleen: I guess I did okay then because they didn't ask me to postpone.

Pat: I wouldn't be so sure. You may have completed your presentation today, but there's no guarantee you'll be invited back. You should have consulted me before the presentation, and I could have told you about the outline. Sometimes you young people just don't think before you act.

Kathleen: I thought I . . .

Pat: That's exactly the problem. You thought! Next time do yourself a favor and come to me first.

Kathleen was wounded for two reasons. First, the feedback Pat offered was uninvited. He didn't ask permission to offer his observations. And Kathleen didn't seek his assistance. Feedback provided without invitation can easily be perceived as unwelcome or unwarranted. Kathleen was not prepared for the feedback and was even more surprised at the corrective nature of Pat's observations. The critical content of Pat's comments, compounded by the surprise of his uninvited observations, resulted in Kathleen's feeling demeaned by the interaction. This unfortunate sequence amounted to a "sneak attack" on the unsuspecting victim. Although short in duration, it is one of the most damaging behaviors possible in the life cycle of a conflict. Kathleen will long remember Pat's criticism and be wary of his intentions in the future. Although this interaction was brief and likely unnoticed by anyone other than Kathleen and Pat, the psychological wound was real and lasting. Kathleen will be inclined to behave in much more cautious ways with Pat. In turn, this may lead to Pat wondering about Kathleen's change in demeanor. The result is a continuing deteriorization of the relationship. Sadly, Pat's demeaning behavior may lead to continuing discomfort and eventually manifest as either a full-blown argument or chronic avoidance.

Another kind of demeaning behavior is misplaced humor or sarcasm that results in pain or embarrassment. Many times we've heard that a demeaning comment or observation was meant only in jest. Yet these quick, piercing jabs can be among the most toxic behaviors in working relationships. What is claimed to be "just kidding" or "just joking around" to the sender might be received as a put-down or criticism by the recipient. And when it comes to managing conflict, these types of demeaning behaviors are certain to enflame the situation.

Hollywood has produced a number of shining examples of those who are skilled in the art of demeaning others through the use of sarcasm and insults. The undisputed "king" of insults was Don Rickles. During his heyday Rickles's "schtick" was an avalanche of insults aimed at members of his audience or his hosts during frequent guest appearances on late-night talk shows. His quickness and delivery were second to none, and his apparent bottomless well of barbs made him one of the most recognizable performers in the world. Audiences came expecting to be insulted. An audience member singled out for a verbal assault by Rickles wore the insult like a badge of honor. Nobody could garner more laughs by calling an innocent bystander a "hockey puck" than Rickles.

Rivaling Rickles as an artist of wit and sarcasm was the character Hawkeye Pierce played by Alan Alda on the all-time favorite television comedy/drama, M.A.S.H. Almost everyone old enough to watch reruns of the now syndicated show can cite a favorite Hawkeye quip at the expense of one his colleagues. Even cloaked in the guise of comedy, Hawkeye often came across as abrasive and usually lived up to the verb form of his name as he slung piercing verbal missiles across the studio's operating room set.

What separates our love and appreciation for the art of Don Rickles and Alan Alda with our abhorrence for similar, if not identical, verbal abuse in the name of humor during everyday life? For one thing, when we are watching Rickles or Alda, we expect to be entertained. There is no context for conflict. Usually when a colleague or coworker uses sarcasm or insults, the expectation is profoundly different and the interpretation completely opposite. Even in the midst of a conflict when the expectation for civil, straight, kind interaction is somewhat lowered, an insult or sarcastic comment can completely crumble any hope of progress. On a related note, expectations lead to one's interpretation of intent. The expectation of humor in Rickles's and Alda's routines provided evidence that their intent was to entertain rather than injure. In the workplace, especially when relationships are weak or strained, even the slightest attempt at humor or sarcasm at your conflict partner's expense can result in misinterpretation and result in a conclusion of malice or poor intent. When the recipient of the "humor" feels slighted, embarrassed, or hurt by the comment, the impact can be enormously damaging.

Our recommendation is to avoid demeaning behavior whether or not there is any threat of conflict. When relationships are strained or a conflict is in progress, resisting the temptation to use sarcasm or humor at another's expense is exceptionally good advice. To avoid humor altogether in the workplace, though, is certainly overkill. Obviously not without risks, well-timed humor can contribute to the relaxation of tension and lead to potentially satisfying outcomes of conflict. But sarcasm and humor that injure another party have no place in the practice of the conflict competent leader.

Finally, Demeaning Others can take the form of nonverbal actions and gestures that communicate displeasure, boredom, disagreement, or other negative connotations. Two examples of classic nonverbal demeaning behavior are described below. We'll be surprised if you are unable to recall being witness to or directly involved in at least one similar instance.

Earlier in this chapter, we reviewed a demeaning interaction between Pat and Kathleen. Pat exhibited demeaning behavior toward Kathleen with his uninvited and harsh criticism regarding her presentation to the executive team. What we did not describe was a moment during Kathleen's presentation when Pat leaked his displeasure that foretold his later criticism. Here's what happened: Kathleen had just been introduced to the team and was standing at the head of the boardroom table. She could feel the anxiety begin to well up in her chest as it did before almost every presentation. This time, though, the stakes were higher. It was her first time presenting to the executive team. She cleared her throat, looked out at the team, and began to speak just as she had rehearsed. She thanked the team for inviting her to present and said, "I've been looking forward to sharing with you the preliminary results of our project. I hope my enthusiasm for this project doesn't overwhelm my ability to present the data clearly. Please feel free to ask me questions at any time."

Feeling better now that she had spoken her first few sentences without stumbling, she reached for her copies of her presentation. Smoothly she divided the stack into two equal parts and handed each to the participants sitting nearest her, saying, "These are copies of my presentation slides for your reference. I hope you find them helpful during the presentation." She noticed the executive team member on her right briefly pause, glance at the handouts, and then raise an eyebrow as if preparing to ask a question. No question was forthcoming, so Kathleen continued with her presentation and the moment passed into the recesses of her memory. Kathleen clicked the remote to display her first slide and began describing the scope of the project. Looking toward the back of the room, she caught the eye of her colleague Pat. Kathleen smiled broadly, then noted that Pat was staring directly at her ever so slightly shaking his head. His eyes looked like slits and his smile was nonexistent, replaced instead by a questioning frown. Momentarily unsure of Pat's intent, Kathleen paused, then refocused on her presentation and continued. Try as she might to avoid looking his way again, she found herself glancing toward his seat and noticed Pat still shaking his head and covering his eyes with his left hand. *What in the world is he trying to tell me?* she thought. *And why is he acting this way at a time like this?* Kathleen felt hurt and suddenly more anxious than before. She continued her presentation without further incident and recalled Pat's behavior only when he approached her at lunch later that day.

Most of us recognize the variety of negative nonverbal cues individuals can display. Arms folded tightly across the chest, head shaking side to side, squinting eyes, and a frowning mouth are some of the signals of disapproval or disagreement. When these or similar behaviors are exhibited during times of anxiety or early in the conflict cycle, the result can be just as strong as a verbal barrage. Pat's behavior struck Kathleen as both a sign of disapproval and a surprise. Kathleen was in the vulnerable position of presenting to a high-level team for the first time. She wanted to make the best impression possible. When Kathleen noticed Pat in the meeting, what she expected from him was some form of nonverbal support. Instead she received a variety of destructive signals that demonstrated disagreement and led to heightened anxiety. In short, she felt troubled and uncertain because of Pat's behavior. Pat's nonverbal expressions caused Kathleen to perform less confidently and created a slight sense of embarrassment or concern that she wasn't being effective in this important presentation. Coupled later with his critical and uninvited feedback at lunch, the combination of his behaviors and actions had a clear demeaning impact on Kathleen.

A second example of nonverbal demeaning behavior is the rolling of one's eyes. This simple but powerful act can bring an unsuspecting conflict partner to a boil within moments. If we could harness the energy produced by this simple gesture, we'd have a potential source of alternative fuel that could revolutionize our way of life! Here's how it works. During a conflict, one partner chooses to disclose an important new fact or perception about the situation. Having taken a risk by this disclosure, the speaker is hopeful that his conflict partner will recognize the risk and acknowledge it. Instead, the response takes the form of eyes rotating to the right or left, then sweeping up to the top of the eye socket with a flourish of raised eyebrows and whites of the eyes flashing in code, "You've got to be kidding me!" The reaction of the disdained speaker is often a combination of anger and embarrassment. The anger is directed at the gall of the conflict partner to be so demeaning. The embarrassment occurs especially when the eye roll is performed in a public setting, and others witness it.

Just as actions speak louder than words, nonverbal demeaning actions sometimes speak louder than demeaning words. In the world of conflict incompetence, nonverbal behaviors can be deadly harbingers of situations that will spiral out of control. Actions that demean others, verbal or nonverbal, are among the most costly anyone can exhibit. They hit the present with painful precision. And their after-effects can linger for months, even years, when left unattended and unresolved.

Retaliating. Perhaps the most basic, almost instinctual active destructive behavior is retaliation. The biblical adage, "an eye for an eye," refers to the concept of ultimate fairness when it comes to retaliation. For someone who is suffering a loss at the hands of an opponent, inflicting an equal loss on the opponent is just. Responding in kind as punishment or in retaliation for one's losses is not only acceptable but fair. Retaliating at an escalated level is presumably unfair and unacceptable.

In today's workplace, there is no fairness in Retaliating, and there is no rational basis for engaging in it. The result of Retaliating is certain and destructive. When practiced, the consequence is continued conflict at a heightened level. Why, then, do we find people in organizations responding in retaliatory ways during conflict? In the fallible world of humanity, some people simply choose poorly. Understanding the potential damage caused by Retaliating is the first step toward controlling the urge to retaliate.

Most retaliatory behavior is associated with unexpressed emotions. When an individual experiences anger, envy, or embarrassment presumably caused by another and keeps those emotions hidden while imagining a payback, the chances for retaliation increase exponentially. Rather than expressing one's emotions in constructive ways, the individual attempts to invoke the "eye for an eye" method to get even. In an "I'll show you" moment, the conflict escalates, and both parties are left to wonder what went wrong. The basic problem is that what one party sees as a step that brings the situation back to "even" is interpreted by the other as a first-time strike or provocation. There is no getting even because each successive retaliation fuels a burgeoning inferno of conflict. Retaliation almost always results in a deteriorating situation. This self-defeating behavior almost always causes mere Differences or Misunderstandings to quickly be transformed into Discord and Polarization.

To illustrate, let's analyze a misunderstanding between two directors in a sales organization called Best Solutions. They are responsible for complementary but separate lines of business. Brad runs a department that customizes his company's standard products for use in clients' special applications. Teri is the director of the unit that sells and delivers the standard products. They have a friendly competition regarding which department brings in more revenue each year. Nevertheless, both work for the overall good of Best Solutions and frequently support each other's initiatives.

Brad has cultivated a relationship with a vice president of a large locally based company, World Wide Shipping. Best Solutions has targeted this company for years but has never been successful in landing it as a client. Brad invited the vice president and two of his staff to lunch and a meeting to discuss their needs for the following year. He knew that the vice president was interested in the kinds of products and services Best Solutions offered. He was not certain, though, how ready World Wide Shipping was to commit. He considered this a big step in cementing the relationship but not necessarily an opportunity to close a deal. Brad invited his boss, Brent, to the lunch but did not invite Teri. He thought it was still too early in the process to involve her and didn't want to waste her time.

Teri learned of the lunch and meeting only when she attempted to reserve the conference room for a staff meeting. She was told the conference room had already been reserved for Brad's meeting with World Wide Shipping and that it would be in use until at least 2:00 P.M. because of the catered lunch. Teri felt overlooked. She wondered why Brad would exclude her. This was a meeting with one of Best Solutions's most coveted potential clients. She and Brad had discussed many times how much World Wide Shipping could mean to their business. It just didn't make any sense to her. "What have I done to upset Brad?" she wondered. "Is there a hidden message in this somewhere?"

Over the next few days, Teri's hurt and wonder began to turn to anger. When she returned from a short business trip later that week, she decided that she would forward her trip report, a standard procedure in the office, to everyone except Brad. Trip reports were appreciated as an effective way to maintain good communication among the departments. Often representatives from one department established leads or made contacts that were important to or best followed up by other departments. This tool was a key link in keeping everyone apprised of new business opportunities. When Brad discovered he had been left off the distribution list for Teri's report, he was initially confused. He also had noticed that Teri had not responded to e-mails or voice mails he sent her while she was traveling. His name was the only one left off the standard distribution list for the report so she would have had to remove it intentionally. Obviously Teri's "oversight" was purposeful. Brad decided that if she wanted to play games, well, then, she better get ready.

A misunderstanding quickly escalates into discord and, potentially, polarization because of assumptions and subsequent retaliation. It is seemingly easy to assume negative intent when none is present. And somehow we forget to communicate about our assumptions or feelings, choosing to follow our assumptions and feelings down a path that leads to destructive behavior such as Retaliating. In the end, both parties lose as the retaliatory cycle deepens and the precipitating event fades into oblivion. Retaliating can result only in continuing pain, embarrassment, waste, and anger. Recovering from the damage of it takes time and effort that's costly to the people involved and to the organization. Brad's not inviting Teri to the meeting with World Wide Shipping was at most a poor decision. Teri's oversight in not including Brad on the trip report was clearly a retaliation and created Discord out of a Misunderstanding. Such retaliatory behavior can lead only to deepening conflict and a potentially long recovery period for the conflict partners.

Passive Destructive Behaviors. The Active Destructive Behaviors of Winning at All Costs, Displaying Anger, Demeaning Others, and Retaliating have no rational place in organizations, yet they appear with a frequency that belies people's intelligence. Unfortunately, part of being human seems to include episodes of behaving poorly when confronting conflict. These behaviors are among the most toxic anyone can choose. Understanding what they are and coming to grips with why people use them are important steps in becoming conflict competent leaders. And just as important is the exploration of Passive Destructive Behaviors.

In contrast to the Active Destructive Behaviors, Passive Destructive Behaviors are those that require little effort and usually involve the person's refraining from some type of action. These kinds of behaviors typically cause the conflict to continue, reach a resolution that is unsatisfactory, or reach a false resolution, and the conflict picks up where it left off. In many cases, the passive nature of these behaviors causes them to go unnoticed. This rather insidious characteristic presents a challenge not only to those involved in the conflict but to leaders embracing the notion of conflict competence.

Avoiding. Think of someone at work with whom you have or have had a conflict. Picture that person in your mind. Think about the interactions you have with this person. Here is a question for you: Do you tend to minimize your time with this person or maximize your time? In other words, do you try to spend more time or less time with him or her? Many, if not most, of us find that we spend less time. And a large percentage of us purposely and consciously find ways to reduce our interactions with the other. When it comes to conflict, we are a veritable society of avoiders.

One of the most common practices for dealing with conflict is not dealing with it at all. Rather than confronting the problem head-on, people choose to ignore the person or the problem, somehow hoping that their inaction will result in an eventual resolution. In our previous discussion of fight-and-flight responses, we described the vestiges of instinct left over from our ancient ancestors. When confronted with situations generating fear or anger, a person's genetic wiring kicks in with fight-or-flight responses. A person's behavior, though, is quite controllable. Although many find it difficult, everyone can choose whether to take action (active behaviors) or avoid action (passive behaviors). Unfortunately, people often choose one of a number of passive, or flight-type, responses to conflict. Many times those passive responses are categorized as avoidance.

Scores of people we interviewed reported that their earliest reaction to conflict is to avoid it. We heard the avoidance sentiment expressed in dozens of creative ways. Here are just a few:

"Why get involved in a spat with someone when you can avoid it? It can only make things worse."

"I've never seen the wisdom in confronting someone when just letting it go usually solves the problem. Why make a bad situation worse by getting all emotional?"

"I was raised to believe that most problems resolve themselves if you just give them a little time."

"I want people to like me. That's not possible if you're in conflict with them."

"I've tried confronting people. Afterwards I find myself worrying about how they're going to get even with me."

"My boss just doesn't handle conflict well. I sure don't want her mad at me. So I do my best to avoid conflict or avoid her."

Why do so many of us choose avoidance? Our experience suggests that at the root of much avoidance is fear, which can take many forms: fear of reprisals, fear of making the situation worse, fear of becoming emotional especially in front of others, fear of losing one's temper, fear of losing face or acceptance, fear of damaging one's reputation, and fear of being wrong. This fear is sometimes expressed as "not liking the way conflict makes me feel." And it is often accompanied by some form of wishful thinking or magical hope that the conflict will resolve itself given enough time.

We submit that the vast majority of fears associated with avoidance are nothing more than myths, conclusions based on poor assumptions, or concerns based in a lack of self-confidence. Consider, for instance, the fear of making the situation worse. Engaging another regarding a Disagreement or Difference may result in overt pronouncements that clearly demonstrate the degree of Disagreement or Difference. The discussion may even include some emotionally charged dialogue. If the differences can be described clearly, though, the chance of a resolution is actually improved, not worsened. In fact, it is only through avoidance that there is a guarantee that the conflict will go unresolved. When a conflict occurs between two or more people, the most effective way to ensure the conflict's continuance is to use avoidance. Then it never goes away.

Another kind of faulty fear is being concerned about becoming emotional or losing one's temper. Losing one's temper is almost never a good idea. An individual who is consistently battling to control his or her temper will likely find conflict particularly challenging. People who have temper issues can benefit from coaching or counseling aimed at discovering the root problem, identifying early signs of temper, and learning tactics that help subdue the emotional outbursts associated with a bad temper. In cases of chronic temper issues, some avoidance behavior may be warranted. These cases, though, are rare and isolated. The related fear of becoming emotional in front of others is not to be taken lightly either. Many people believe experiencing emotion is harmful during conflict. However, as we'll explore in more depth later, almost the exact opposite is true. Sharing emotions (versus hiding them) has been shown to be constructive and valuable in conflict resolution. In fact, hiding emotions is very difficult, if not impossible, to do effectively on a consistent basis. In most cases, the very emotion you may be attempting to hide leaks out through nonverbal behaviors or bursts out at an inopportune moment. The very fear that people have been trying to stifle by avoiding conflict may quite possibly be realized through these leaks or bursts. So the wisdom of avoidance as protection from becoming emotional is actually one of the worst tactics to employ.

The fears of losing face, damaging one's reputation, and being wrong are closely related. Again, the tactic of avoidance most often backfires on the person trying to mitigate these fears. During conflict, the chronic avoider only adds to his or her reputation as an avoider, that is, someone who consistently refuses to engage in dialogue or debate the issues. Avoiders are seldom sought out for their ideas. Their reputation is often one of self-centeredness and self-preservation, and lacking in initiative. Why would anyone fear damaging this kind of reputation? Losing face during a conflict is possible, but usually only in conflicts that are mishandled. Handled effectively, the vast majority of conflicts are opportunities to discover and learn. The fear of being wrong is, we suppose, a valid concern, but only in those dinosaurs of organizations where there is no tolerance for making mistakes. Discovering that you are wrong is one of life's best learning opportunities. In the daily course of events that arise in organizations, we salute the notion that conflicts should be embraced. We endorse the concept of searching out those who have views differing from our own. And we hope to discover not just that we are wrong now and then, but that in our wrongness, we find new and stimulating perspectives that enable us to grow and contribute in novel and exciting ways. Fear of being wrong? On the contrary, we suggest that people can learn and grow when they are wrong.

Conflict competent leaders learn that avoidance itself has many negative consequences. Most organizations recognize and reward people for demonstrating initiative, solving problems, being decisive, and taking action. Similarly, organizations take a dim view of people who show no initiative, avoid making decisions, and do only what is necessary. Overcoming learned avoidance behavior is critical not only for improving the ability to deal with conflict, but also for improving how we are viewed in the organization.

Yielding. Closely related to Avoiding, Yielding is another form of choosing inaction over action. The act of Yielding occurs when a person decides to "give in" to another's wish, idea, or viewpoint even though he or she sees the situation or solution differently. Some of the very same fears associated with avoidance are at the root of reasons people choose to yield. They do not want to lose face or damage their reputation. They fear being wrong. They may not want to look bad to others or believe that others think that their ideas or views are less than solid. Some yield because they cannot tolerate any form of conflict. Just as with avoidance, most of these fears are not only rooted in a lack of self-confidence, but the very act of Yielding is often self-defeating in that their fears may be realized because they yield.

Yielding behavior may be commonly associated with people giving in to those they perceive as having more position power. In other words, people may believe they yield most frequently to those at higher levels or positions in the company. This may be true for some. In our investigation of how and why people exhibit conflict behaviors, we found that those who yield most frequently tend to do so across many levels in the organization. Others yield more situationally, depending not only on the perceived positional power of their conflict partner but also on their own perceived personal power.

Vincent was a rising star in his company, a marketing agency. He was young and enthusiastic and brought a passion to his role of creative consultant that not many had seen recently. When left to his own devices, he came up with ideas that were sometimes so clever that his coworkers could barely keep up. Vincent began to gain a reputation among some, though, that he was more concerned about himself than he was a team player. When confronted with this perception or challenged by others, Vincent usually hung his head, muttered an apology, and disappeared as quickly as he could. JT, Vincent's boss, was a bit of an "old school" manager. He recruited only those he thought would fit with the rest of the team yet would raise the productivity of the team at the same time. Hard work and loyalty were critical. He demanded that employees focus their efforts in ways that made the team better. Those looking for individual notoriety and recognition would not last long on JT's team.

Vincent's productivity and his reputation for creativity and innovation grew quickly. JT recognized Vincent's talent yet continued to demand that Vincent demonstrate restraint and contribute to the team without flash and independence. Vincent appreciated his colleagues and the success of the team but felt that JT's controlling methods stifled not only his own creativity but the potential productivity of the entire department. Their conflict grew. JT, always the extroverted leader, continued to demand team play, heaped praise on those deserving it, and openly criticized those who didn't contribute. Vincent, never one for confrontation, refused to push for more freedom. In addition, out of respect for JT's leadership and regard for his teammates, he continued to yield to JT. He labored to repress his growing disdain for JT's methods yet steadfastly refrained from engaging in any debate with JT. Vincent confided in a few close friends that he was growing more and more frustrated. He described his frustration as "feeling like I'm going to just up and quit one day over something JT says even if it's not the real issue. I don't want to take him on because he's my boss, and you just don't fight with your boss. I have to admit he is nothing if not fair and treats everyone the same. But I feel that every time I get creative, he just squashes me. I don't know how much longer I can take it."

The issue between JT and Vincent eventually was resolved, but not without pain and consternation. Vincent seriously contemplated leaving the company. Upper management grew concerned that some unrest was forming in JT's department. JT thought that Vincent might be undermining his authority by complaining to others, and he had noticed lower productivity from Vincent. The resolution was made possible only after Vincent decided he could no longer conceal his concerns and follow JT's lead without question. With much encouragement from his friends, he finally spoke with JT privately. True to form, during the meeting, Vincent said he was out of line for bringing up his concerns and suggested they just forget the issue. JT insightfully concluded, though, that the problem was real. They determined that they could not resolve the issues by themselves and involved other parties from the organization to help them sort through their issues.

JT and Vincent are still working together years later, so there is a happy ending. Had Vincent overcome his Yielding behavior earlier in their relationship, though, the conflict may not have grown as severe and the productivity of the team may not have suffered as long. In this case, some of the very reasons Vincent chose to yield (out of respect for JT's leadership position and the good of the team) bore the brunt of the difficulties experienced during the conflict. Vincent began to question JT's authority as the conflict festered. The team suffered as Vincent and JT never seemed in synch. Yielding felt like the best course of action to Vincent. Yet his reluctance to engage JT for so long yielded only a continuing and deepening conflict.

Conflict competent leaders yield judiciously. To say that no one should ever yield is not only an exaggeration but is potentially destructive. In our previous discussion of Active Destructive Behaviors, Winning at All Costs was one of the four problematic categories. Those who never yield are likely seen as people who attempt Winning at All Costs. This is a case of two Destructive Behaviors being clearly and logically linked.

Conflict competent leaders are also adept at spotting those in their organization who yield on a regular basis. They offer advice and support to "yielders" in the hope that they will learn to take more active stances when dealing with conflict. They do this in the name of encouraging healthy debate and expanding the creativity of the organization through debate and dialogue. Had a conflict competent leader observed the situation between Vincent and JT, he or she may have been in a position to provide feedback and encouragement to Vincent regarding his behavior earlier in the conflict. Early intervention may have enabled a quicker, less painful resolution. It most certainly would have reduced Vincent's frustration and encouraged more productive behaviors for dealing with this conflict and other conflicts in the future.

Hiding Emotions. Avoiding, Yielding, and Hiding Emotions are all related. They share the common characteristic of withholding feelings, thoughts, and ideas. In all three cases, the withholding is likely related to a person's fears regarding how he or she will be perceived by others or a lack of confidence regarding the ability to engage effectively in the conflict. In the example, Vincent clearly attempted to hide his emotions throughout the conflict with JT. Behaviorally, he had some success in keeping his emotions out of JT's view. Internally, though, Vincent's resentment toward JT grew. As is usually the case with Hiding Emotions, it became difficult to suppress his emotions. He began sharing his frustration with coworkers and eventually raised concern among others in the organization.

Emotions, especially when withheld over a significant length of time, have a tendency to leak out. Sometimes, as in the case with Vincent, the emotions leak through sharing with people other than one's conflict partner. This can appear to others as complaining, whining, or talking about others behind their backs, all of which carry negative consequences and continue to fuel the conflict.

In other cases, the leakage takes forms that resemble some of the Active Destructive behaviors discussed earlier. One way is through the use of nonverbal behaviors that are noticeable by others but perhaps undetected by the sender. These nonverbal cues can appear to others as forms of Demeaning Others, one of the most powerful Active Destructive behaviors. Another leakage is characterized by sudden and unexpected outbursts of pent-up emotion, sometimes triggered by seemingly insignificant issues. This is akin to the straw that broke the camel's back. When it happens, others often perceive the behavior as Displaying Anger. When the outburst or overflow of hidden emotion takes the form of sarcasm or criticism, it also can appear as Demeaning Others. In still other cases, the behavior may take the form of Retaliating.

While there is value in not expressing every emotion we feel in a conflict, hiding relevant feelings or concerns can lead to a number of issues. Among these are less trusting relationships with co-workers and the perception of questionable commitment to the organization. In addition, unexpressed or suppressed emotions can lead to a variety of personal health issues, including depression, insomnia, and headaches (Capobianco, Davis, and Kraus, 1999). At the very least, concealing emotions is costly in terms of the energy it takes to keep the feeling inside, which often leads to discomfort or stress.

Perhaps the most telling problem with Hiding Emotions during conflict is the way in which a conflict partner perceives it. As effective as some of us are in concealing our emotions, most of us are even better at discerning small telltale signs that another is not giving us the whole story. Straightforward, honest communication is the backbone of solid, trusting relationships. Conflict competent leaders build relationships based on trust and deal with conflict effectively in large part due to this trust. When someone is perceived as withholding feelings or information, it is not much of a stretch to question that person's motives, sincerity, and honesty. Such is the case with Virginia and Ann.

Virginia is the chief operating officer (COO) of a major public power company. Ann is a vice president in charge of communications and public relations. Virginia has been in the business her entire career, working her way up the ladder. She has been part of several mergers and always gained the respect and admiration of her colleagues through her work ethic, openness, and vision for constantly improving service for customers. Virginia seldom pulls punches and is known for her passion for honest and complete communication. Ann has significant experience outside the industry and joined the power company seven years ago as the director of public relations. She was promoted to her current position two years ago and has enjoyed solid working relationships with Virginia and other members of the executive staff. Ann is known for her ability to handle stressful situations and has gained a reputation for her calming presence with consumers and her smooth confidence when dealing with the media.

During an executive staff meeting, Ann discussed the press conference and interviews she gave to local media outlets regarding the company's request for a rate increase. Obviously rate increases are never popular with consumers. Ann believes the press relishes these opportunities to make the company look greedy, especially when the rate increases come on the heels of natural disasters. The interviews went well despite the tough questioning. Ann reported with some pride that nobody should be worried about what the late-night news would show that night. She could not recall a series of interviews that had gone so well. The press conference had also gone well, although she was not pleased with one section of the report she distributed that detailed the expenses incurred during power restoration efforts. She was concerned that some of the estimates seemed overstated, but did not address this during the press conference or the interviews. Since no reporter had asked about the estimates, she quickly dismissed her concerns and decided no follow-up was needed. Ann did not mention this to the executive staff.

As she concluded her report to the staff and invited questions, Ann felt confident that she had represented the company well and expected her colleagues to feel the same way. Several staff members lauded her efforts and thanked her profusely. Virginia also felt good about Ann's report, but had not heard enough about the press conference. She recalled past instances when she thought Ann's spin on issues was just a little too positive. In this case, she thought Ann emphasized the interviews during her report much more than the press conference and decided to check. "Ann," she said, "you seemed very pleased with the interviews. Were you equally pleased with the press conference?"

Ann thought Virginia's question seemed a bit out of place given the overall approval she'd experienced from the staff. But Virginia always asked insightful and sometimes tough questions. Ann responded that no problems were evident during the press conference. Had there been any, she assured the staff, she would have been grilled about them during the interviews. Virginia smiled and agreed that was true. "But that wasn't my question. I was wondering if you were as pleased with the press conference as you were with the interviews." Ann now felt a bit put on the spot. Virginia always had a way of making her feel somewhat uncomfortable with her questions. But she reminded herself that she was a pro and would not let anybody see her sweat. Ann again reassured Virginia and the staff that she felt very good about the press conference. Virginia reiterated that this request for a rate increase needed to be treated with greater sensitivity than most other requests because of the recent storm recovery. She also suggested that the executive staff needed to know "if there was even a hint of concern." Ann's feeling of being on the spot now began to give way to feeling accused, and she began to grow irritated. Virginia noticed a change in Ann's tone as she continued to respond to her questions. "Public relations people are so hard to read," Virginia thought to herself. "I wish she would just tell us what she thinks. There's no reason to hide anything. And if she's upset with my insistence, she should say so. Why can't I ever seem to trust her to tell me the whole story?" After a few more minutes of Virginia's questions and Ann's reassurances, the meeting adjourned. Ann left wondering why Virginia always put her on the spot. Virginia left certain that Ann could never be fully straight with her or the executive staff and therefore could never be fully trusted.

This episode demonstrates the most insidious result of Hiding Emotions. When we attempt to keep emotions hidden, others are likely to pick up on subtle cues that signal some discomfort or uneasiness. This often leads to doubts about honesty, and trust begins to erode. When there is a lack of trust between conflict partners, the potential for successful resolution is seriously diminished.

Self-Criticizing. The ability to conduct an accurate self-appraisal is critical to personal growth and development. Understanding what we do well provides confidence for drawing on that ability during challenging times. Understanding what we do not do so well provides clarity and priority about areas for development. When we find that our self-appraisal becomes severely negative, however, it is possible that such negativity can result in the final Destructive Behavior we will discuss, Self-Criticizing behavior.

Self-Criticizing is most evident after a conflict has occurred. There are both internal and external signs. Think about a time when you have had a conflict with a coworker and found yourself replaying the incident over and over in your head. You may recall that you found yourself thinking about the conflict well after the interaction has concluded. You may remember the incident dominating your thoughts to the extent of daydreaming about it. It is possible that you even lost sleep over it, lying awake at night because you could not get it out of your head. If you have ever experienced any of these symptoms, you know how Self-Criticizing can affect your internal psyche. Beyond the waste of time and focus, overly self-critical behavior can also lead to a variety of stress-induced ailments such as insomnia, depression, or even panic attacks (Capobianco, Davis, and Kraus, 1999).

The external evidence of Self-Criticizing may be more obvious to observers than to the person exhibiting the behaviors. For instance, he or she may dwell on minor mistakes or conflicts in ways that become annoying to others. People may apologize over and over for miscues that the other party has long since forgiven or forgotten. Individuals may constantly refer to an incident or conflict in an effort to somehow find an absolutely perfect solution, even when the other party is already satisfied with the outcome. The bottom line is that some people cannot seem to let the issue go and continue to blame themselves for issues or behaviors that appear entirely out of proportion to the actual circumstances.

One possible source of self-critical behavior is setting unrealistically high standards for oneself. When the goals or standards are not met, the person is incredibly tough on himself or herself. This person frequently dwells on unmet goals and seldom takes credit for reaching goals or positive outcomes. As the unrealistically high goals are perpetuated, the cycle of self-criticism continues unabated.

Another possible reason for overly self-critical behavior is previous experience with a boss or parent or other authority figure who was extraordinarily tough or demanding. It is possible in this case that the standards demanded by the authority figure have influenced the person to set inordinately high standards for himself or herself. The cycle of self-critical behavior starts and continues as described.

However it starts, this behavior is identified as destructive because it contributes to conflicts' continuing or lasting longer than necessary. It wastes time and energy and maintains a focus on issues that are no longer important or relevant. Unchecked, it can cause the individual to grossly overestimate the gravity of conflict situations and perpetuate conflicts unnecessarily. The trademark of the penultimate self-criticizer is never being happy with a successful outcome. Ultimately, self-criticism can cause working relationships to dissolve for no reason other than that the person becomes too miserable to be around. Conflict resolution suffers because the self-critical person is never happy with an outcome, never satisfied that his or her conflict partner is satisfied, and never pleased with his or her performance before, during, or after the conflict.

Summary

When conflict occurs, there are a myriad of ways people can behave that perpetuate or worsen the conflict. We identify these as Destructive Behaviors. We hope the examples we've cited and situations we've described help to illustrate the ease with which we all can fail to embrace conflict in positive ways. No one is perfect. Everyone encounters conflict situations to which people respond with less than spectacular behavior. The point is that people can choose better responses to conflict with just a little more self-awareness, analysis, patience, and practice. Conflict competent leaders are those who can detect Destructive Behaviors in themselves and others, take steps to correct the behaviors, and encourage behaviors, practices, and processes that enable successful resolution to conflict. When this occurs in consistent ways in organizations, conflict can become a valuable source of creativity and problem solving. Conflict competent leaders replace Destructive Behaviors with Constructive Behaviors consistently. As we will see in Chapter Five, the practice of Constructive Behaviors is not only the antithesis of Destructive Behaviors; it can be the foundation of personal and organizational success in ways previously unimagined and unrealized.

5

FOSTERING CONSTRUCTIVE RESPONSES TO CONFLICT

Could a greater miracle take place than for us to
look through each other's eyes for an instant?
—*Henry David Thoreau*

Leaders are leaders not because they have a title or a position. They are leaders because of what they do and how they do it. How people conduct themselves routinely, the way they act in challenging circumstances, and the manner in which they behave toward others provide the basis on which others view them. Many people behave in ways that others find acceptable. A few behave consistently in ways that transcend acceptability and propel them to leadership. People have been establishing themselves as leaders throughout history. The foundations of leadership have been explored and researched for decades. Leadership development practices have been chronicled and applied for nearly as long. The study of conflict and conflict resolution has been a much more recent development even though conflict has been part of human existence just as long as leadership.

Our contention is that the most effective leaders are extraordinarily competent at handling conflict. In this chapter, we examine specific ways they respond to conflict constructively. In so doing, they not only keep potentially damaging situations under control, they discover options, solutions, and possibilities previously unseen or unknown. They learn to embrace conflict not as an organizational enemy but as an opportunity for growth and a source of creative energy.

We reviewed in Chapter Four the intensity levels associated with conflict and eight kinds of behaviors that lead to continued or escalated conflict. With so much that can so easily go askew with conflict, how much hope is there that conflict can be handled effectively on a consistent basis? Actually, we think that there is just as much, if not more, that can go right with conflict. And when things go right, the payoffs are enormous.

We start by reviewing five ways effective leaders encourage positive responses to conflict. Then we analyze seven specific behaviors, or Constructive Responses, that leaders practice before, during, and after conflict.

Weathering the Storm of Conflict

In the annals of history, many of the most respected leaders are those remembered best for how they rose to meet daunting challenges or prevailed in the face of seemingly insurmountable odds. Abraham Lincoln is revered for helping a nation survive a catastrophic conflict of philosophies. Winston Churchill is famous for pulling his country through a brutal siege and standing up to the fear and anxiety brought on by seemingly endless attacks. Martin Luther King Jr. is memorialized for his strength of character and unwillingness to support violent tactics in the face of injustice and unfair treatment. Each of these leaders faced conflicts of a scale that most of us can hardly fathom and will likely never experience. What defined them is how they responded in times of conflict. And what may very well define today's leaders in organizations around the world is how they respond in times of conflict. Because conflict is inevitable and frequent, conflict competent leaders must rise to the occasion on a daily basis.

Staying Calm in the Face of Conflict

Who doesn't admire the person who handles a crisis with a sense of confidence and calmness? Who doesn't envy the person who is composed and at ease in the middle of an argument? Who isn't mesmerized watching Henry Fonda starring in the classic *Twelve Angry*

Men as he casts the only not-guilty vote in the jury room? Not everyone can appear cool, calm, and collected under fire. In fact, the biological changes in one's body during times of high stress often result in the exact opposite of calmness. So what can we do, if anything, to improve our ability to stay calm in the face of conflict? We offer several suggestions.

• *Make a list.* Many people have several triggers or hot buttons that, when encountered, lead to intense emotional responses. Think about the times you've lost your composure, and then write down what caused your loss. Just make a list, without evaluating anything. Keep writing until you fill up a page (aim for twenty to thirty items). Now look over your list; see if you can find similarities among any of the items, and begin grouping them into categories. Do certain people make your list more than once? Do certain kinds of people make the list? Certain events or kinds of events? Places? Times? As you organize your list into categories, you might ask yourself why you respond poorly to these situations or people, and try to think of alternative responses. Ultimately the key is being able to access alternative responses when confronted with a trigger. The result is that you not only appear calmer, but you actually may feel calmer too.

• *Count to ten.* No doubt you have heard this advice since you were old enough to count that high. The reason this is good advice goes back to those pesky glands that release adrenaline and other hormones into your body that put you on high alert. The hormones do their job well every time. Their one shortcoming, thankfully, is that their effects get diluted relatively quickly. If you can delay your response for a minute or so, it is likely that the most intense adrenaline-induced response urges will have worn off. Now you can choose your response without so much interference from inside your body. Of course, there are lots of other delay tactics as well. You can excuse yourself to make a trip to the rest room. You can refill your coffee. You could look over your notes (or pretend to look them over). You could even say, "Do you mind if I take a quick break? I'll be right back." Almost any delay will help take the edge off the adrenaline rush and put you more in control of your responses.

- *Just the facts*. Sergeant Joe Friday of *Dragnet* fame always urged his witnesses to report "just the facts, ma'am, just the facts." It was his way of helping people who may have witnessed a disturbing situation remain calm and recall important details that could help solve the crime. In much the same way, when you feel the first hint of anxiety or stress, you might want to clarify what has been said, check your understanding, or summarize what has been covered. These tactics help focus on facts or previously stated information and steer clear of focusing on people or emotions. It also may help avoid any suggestion of blame during a conflict. And it buys you a little more time to collect your thoughts and delay potentially harmful responses.

- *Understand; then conclude*. My (Tim's) family owns all six *Star Wars* movies. My daughter owns thirty or more *Star Wars* books, several *Star Wars* games, and numerous posters and T-shirts. So when I proudly announced that I was quoting Yoda in this book, I was sure I had succeeded in endearing myself to her in a most significant way. Unfortunately, when I asked her to confirm the quotation's accuracy and authenticity, she informed me that I was sadly mistaken. So with apologies to my daughter, George Lucas, and Steven Spielberg, another way to stay calm during conflict is to follow the advice of Yoda as he *might* have suggested to Luke Skywalker: "Jump to conclusions not, young master."

Many people in their scramble to put a rapid end to conflict accept a quick conclusion or first solution. This rush to judgment can not only result in a poor-quality resolution but can also be a sign of anxiety or stress induced by the conflict. Several more effective alternatives include exploring the situation, considering options, hearing others out, clarifying, and debating. People appear calmer and more thoughtful, considerate, and deliberate as they explore, consider, listen, clarify, and debate. Furthermore, better conclusions will result.

Effective leaders get high marks for their ability (or their perceived ability) to remain calm under duress. Composure and self-control are valuable strengths that give followers confidence that their leaders will deal with conflict and stressful situations successfully. Finding ways to improve your ability to be calm and to appear calm will provide an added degree of self-confidence for dealing with conflicts that arise. The suggestions provided above can help you get started.

Encouraging Civility, Fairness, and Safety

Nothing impairs the ability to handle conflict more severely than the appearance of unfair treatment or concerns for one's safety. By *safety*, we mean several things. Certainly safety includes feeling secure from threats or physical harm. This kind of safety should never be compromised in the workplace. Another kind of safety is the type that makes it possible to discuss even the most troubling situations or information. When it's safe, people can say or discuss anything (Patterson, Grenny, McMillan, and Switzler, 2002). Those best at communication during conflict are very good at spotting safety issues that prevent or disrupt the free flow of ideas. These issues are often disguised as fight-or-flight behaviors. People may raise their voices, retaliate, or refute out of anger (fight). They sometimes shut down, withdraw, or avoid out of fear (flight). In either case, safety has been compromised. It's no longer safe for the free flow of discussion and dialogue. Unfortunately, when the conflict approaches its highest intensities, Discord and Polarization, the likelihood of unfairness or safety concerns increases substantially.

Conflict competent leaders not only encourage civility, fairness, and safety; they demand it. Recalling the rather dire situation involving Renee and James, the pharmaceutical sales team leaders described in Chapter Four, let's see how a conflict competent leader would ensure civility in this continuing conflict.

Over the past few months, Renee and James's relationship had become increasingly antagonistic. During meetings when new guidelines were discussed, they could barely hide their disdain for one another. Steely glares across the table were commonplace, and they often exchanged sharp words. Their boss, Patricia, the regional manager, decided it was time to intervene. She was concerned that the conflict had grown to a level where it no longer was just a dispute between two competent and competitive professionals. It was clear from their behavior in meetings that their disagreements were not going away. She heard from others that the two had exchanged words after the previous meeting. Patricia preferred that her team members, especially her team leaders, work out their differences on their own. Seeing no evidence of progress, she decided it was time to take action.

Patricia decided to speak with James and Renee individually about her observations and concerns. During her meetings, she made it clear that her purpose at this point was not to explore the details of their conflict, to mediate, or to impose a solution. She would leave the resolution up to them. Her purpose was to provide feedback to both of them on the behaviors she had observed and the impact of those behaviors on others and herself. She also intended to encourage them to create time to discuss their differences. Specifically she described the verbal exchanges she had witnessed, the emphatic gestures and other nonverbal behaviors she had observed during meetings, and the rumors she had heard about additional clashes unrelated to meetings. She made it clear that she expected them to stop treating each other poorly, especially in public. She also made it clear that the only way to resolve their conflict was to begin with an agreement for respecting each other's views and working to understand each other's perspectives. Patricia said that as their leader, she was instituting one rule that James and Renee must follow in their discussions: at all times, both must treat the other with respect and fairness. Demeaning tactics and insults were expressly forbidden. She also empathized that the conflict must be a difficult one for both to have expressed such destructive behavior. She assured them that she had the utmost confidence in them in spite of their recent difficulties. Finally, Patricia also offered to meet with them together if they could not make progress meeting on their own.

The steps Patricia took do not ensure that the conflict between Renee and James will be resolved. Her message is, however, a clear signal that a continuance of disrespectful or threatening behavior will not be tolerated. Leaders cannot condone or tolerate uncivil, unfair, or threatening behavior in the workplace. When evidence of such behavior arises, the conflict competent leader takes action. Sometimes the action is to set clear expectations regarding acceptable behavior during times of conflict. Sometimes the action directly addresses the destructive behaviors so that progress in dealing with the conflict is possible. The key is that conflict competent leaders intervene whenever they observe that civility, fairness, or safety is threatened.

Teaching and Coaching Effective Responses

Effective leaders share a penchant for coaching and developing others. A common description of the major difference between managers and leaders is that managers get things done while leaders teach others to get things done. Conflict competent leaders teach, coach, and develop others who are also conflict competent.

One of the strongest impacts that leaders can have on others is to model effective behavior. Leading by example is as powerful today as it ever was. When our leaders say one thing but do another, we almost always question the veracity of their words. In large part, this book addresses leaders' behaviors relative to conflict and suggests that the most effective leaders use Constructive Behaviors while minimizing Destructive Behaviors. Leaders who practice the use of Constructive Behaviors are setting an example toward which others can aspire. When a leader handles a challenging conflict situation effectively, it can inspire and encourage the observer to use similar behaviors and tactics when she faces similar circumstances.

The most effective conflict competent leaders are overt in their actions when it comes to teaching and coaching others. The most effective we have observed are adept at providing feedback, asking questions, empathizing, developing ideas, seeking information, checking for understanding, summarizing, demonstrating behaviors, intervening when necessary, and offering advice. It seems that a careful blend of these techniques works best. Just as with coaching and teaching other leadership competencies, the most successful leaders ply their skills in ways that encourage those in conflict to persevere through the challenge.

Let's continue our review of the conflict between James and Renee. Previously we observed how Patricia encouraged the two to proceed with civility and fairness while addressing their conflict. Now we'll see how Patricia provides coaching during a meeting with James:

> *Patricia:* I'm glad we were able to find time to meet today, James. I've been concerned about the working relationship between you and Renee for a while now.
>
> *James:* I know you're concerned, Patricia. And you should be. Especially with Renee. I'm telling you she is just way out in left field. I don't get it.
>
> *Patricia:* It's clear that the two of you are having some real difficulty. Based on what I've seen and what others have observed, I'd say the conflict between the two of you has evolved well beyond a disagreement or an isolated argument. I think it's affecting not only the two of you, but also your teams and the support staff. We've got to find a way to turn this around.
>
> *James:* So you've actually seen us arguing? And other people are talking about us?
>
> *Patricia:* Yes, I'm afraid so. I can give you specifics if you like.
>
> *James:* (hanging his head) No, you don't have to do that. I know we've gone at it publicly several times recently. Man, she really ticks me off.
>
> *Patricia:* Let's talk about that. You say she really makes you angry. How does that happen?
>
> *James:* For one thing, she's so ultracompetitive. She can't stand that we've beaten her for last six months in sales call volume. Now she's lobbying for changes in the guidelines that would

work to her advantage just so her team could win. That's simply ludicrous!

Patricia: I can tell it bothers you. What about it makes you angry?

James: It's just so juvenile. The friendly competition among sales teams is supposed to be just that: friendly. She's taking it to a whole different level with her whining about "the rules"—you know, the guidelines for what constitutes a sales call. C'mon, who cares about which sales team has the most calls. In the end, it's all about converting sales calls into business.

Patricia: It sounds as if you care.

James: (after a pause) Yeah. I guess I do care about it. It's motivating to my team. We all want to be number one.

Patricia: And I suppose that goes for Renee and her team too. They would like to be number one.

James: Sure. I guess so. They wouldn't be very good salespeople if they didn't. But that still doesn't give her the right to be so petty. Do you know that she actually tells other people lies about me? What is it about her anyway?

Patricia: You really are upset with her. I'd like to hear more about the pettiness in your conflict. I'm sure you have examples of Renee behaving that way.

James: I have plenty of examples. How much time do you have?

Patricia: (smiling) Well, what I'd like to hear are some examples of how you think you may have looked petty to her. Do you think it's possible she may see you that way?

James: What? I thought we were talking about how she's caused this mess.

Patricia: In my experience, I've found that when conflicts become this hot, both parties share some responsibility. And as difficult as it might be, if both parties can look objectively at their own behavior, they often can see how their actions might be perceived as damaging to their conflict partner. I'd like you give it a try. What do you say?

James: You're the boss. And frankly, I'm tired of the conflict. So what do I have to do?

Patricia: Simply this. I'd like you to think of a time that you know you angered Renee and tell me about it.

James: Well, to be honest, there are probably a few. (pausing to think) Okay, there was a problem just last week where she wanted to use the large conference room. I had booked it a couple of weeks in advance for a phone call and a meeting. Well, the meeting fell through. I still had the phone call, though. Renee came to me at the last minute and wanted me to move to the small conference room. She had several people coming in and needed a meeting room large enough to accommodate them. I told her I couldn't move. I think I made up some lame excuse. But mostly I just wanted her to suffer a little. She never would have switched for me, you know.

Patricia: I appreciate your telling me this story. How do you think she remembers this incident?

James: (takes a deep breath) She probably thinks I was being petty and scornful.

Patricia: And were you?

James: Yeah. I was.

Patricia: James, I really do appreciate your willingness to discuss this. Being involved in a conflict this deep is taxing. Your effort to see things from Renee's perspective is a big step in moving toward resolution. It won't be easy. But I believe if you both are willing to work on it this way, there's a real chance that things can improve.

Having a coaching conversation with someone involved in a conflict can be a challenge. In many cases, especially those in which the conflict has reached Discord or Polarization, the person will be defensive and will wish to focus on the shortcomings of the conflict partner. Successful coaches will enable and guide the person with whom they are talking toward an analysis of their own behavior. As we have observed in Patricia's interaction with James, she was able to help James see how he contributed to the conflict with Renee. Although the conflict has a long way to go in order to reach an agreeable resolution, Patricia's skillful use of coaching has initiated a turn in the right direction. Her continued support and guidance will be necessary for both parties as they accept the challenge to resolve their issues.

In Chapter Six, we'll discuss the role coaching plays as conflict competent leaders work to establish effective conflict management systems in their organizations. Credible leaders use their coaching and mentoring prowess to assist and support those in conflict. The more leaders are effective at coaching, mentoring, and mediating, the more likely it is for an organization to maintain a viable conflict management system.

Providing Learning Opportunities

Conflict competent leaders cannot be the exclusive coach for every learner. Certainly they look for opportunities to teach and coach, but it's just as critical that they offer opportunities for development. This can be accomplished in several ways.

The most frequent reason people choose to participate in the courses we offer at LDI is that they have been referred by others. Leaders have suggested that subordinates attend to help them address a conflict with which they've been struggling. Past participants have recommended to peers that they attend so they can share the experience and use the techniques to expand their opportunities when problem solving or resolving conflict. The point is that conflict competent leaders know that learning how to handle conflict is critical for being successful in any organization. One way to learn is by attending classes and training programs designed for this purpose.

Attending training programs, though, is not necessarily the best way or the only way to develop skills for handling conflict. Training programs for any leadership competency are most useful for establishing self-awareness, learning some basic techniques, practicing them, and making plans for applying knowledge and techniques when back at work. Training programs alone are not the most effective venues for real learning and development. The best developmental opportunities come with experience. Leaders can be instrumental in identifying those opportunities, providing support and encouragement during the opportunities, and debriefing with the participant after the learning opportunity.

This is not to suggest that leaders look for just any conflict situation in which to dump their protégés. With any development experience, the right combination of challenge and support is critical for successful learning. Certainly leaders can and should provide suitably challenging experiences for others. And given the right circumstances, leaders can put their protégés in situations that require the use of conflict resolution skills. That said, conflict is a normally occurring and inevitable phenomenon in the workplace. It is likely that during almost any developmental assignment, conflict will occur. The key is how the leader chooses to challenge and support their protégés during such experiences.

As an example, let's revisit the conflict between Harriet, the elementary school principal, and Jeanne, a guidance counselor at the school. Jeanne recently filed a report citing her belief that one of the students may be the victim of abuse. A disagreement ensued when Harriet, after reviewing Jeanne's report, decided that no further action was warranted.

Jeanne was very disappointed with Harriet's decision and decided to speak to the district supervisor for student support services. Jeanne's daily direct reporting relationship is to Harriet, but her reporting relationship for education and development purposes is to the district supervisor, Nancy.

Nancy listened carefully to Jeanne's description of the situation with the student, her handling of the report, and her discussion with the principal. She knew that Jeanne was concerned with Harriet's decision. Nancy guessed that Jeanne was looking for agreement with and support of lodging an official protest. She recognized Jeanne's frustration and complimented her dedication to and concern for her students. Nancy also asked Jeanne many questions about the circumstances: how well Jeanne knew the student, how well Harriet knew the student, how long Jeanne had been working with the student, in what capacity she had come to know the student, what else the student's file indicated about the student's situation, how well she and Harriet had worked together in the past, and others. Throughout the conversation, Nancy made sure to balance her questions with appreciation and support while being careful not to unilaterally agree with Jeanne's position.

Jeanne felt supported by Nancy, but knew also that she was carefully considering all the possibilities connected to the situation. Even as the conversation unfolded, Jeanne began to realize that she did not have all the answers to Nancy's questions and therefore might not have all the information she needed to draw conclusions. So when Nancy asked Jeanne what she could do to understand the student's situation and Harriet's decision better, Jeanne already knew that she needed to schedule an appointment with Harriet to review all that had happened.

If Jeanne had been resistant, Nancy may have needed to suggest that Jeanne schedule a time to speak to Harriet again to review the matter. In this case, the use of simple, focused questions were all that was necessary to lead Jeanne to that same conclusion. Nancy, although she did not directly provide the developmental experience for Jeanne, was instrumental in enabling Jeanne to reassess her actions and decide to reengage Harriet to resolve their differences.

This kind of interaction is a prime example of how a conflict competent leader provides learning opportunities for others. Learning opportunities are not always of the formal variety, like recommending a class or suggesting a reading. Leaders have opportunities to encourage others to face adversity, make assignments that include personal challenges, and insist that others take action. The key for transforming such circumstances into learning opportunities is the leader's ability to provide support for the learner in confronting the challenging situation.

Embracing Constructive Conflict

When asked to create a list of some of the greatest leaders of all time, many of the groups with whom we work suggest a number of people over and over. John Kennedy, Martin Luther King Jr., and Mahatma Gandhi routinely make the list. When asked to identify characteristics or traits of these leaders that propel them to the top of the list, invariably descriptors such as vision, confidence, passion, and enthusiasm are cited. We believe those same traits are critical for changing the way we think about conflict. Leaders who have vision regarding conflict know that conflict can be the catalyst to breakthrough ideas and novel approaches to organizational issues. Those who demonstrate confidence when confronting conflict inspire trust and optimism among their followers. Leaders who are passionate about their beliefs and are just as passionate about understanding others' views are admired for their ability and willingness to consider every angle. And those who show enthusiasm for differing views ("Great, you see it differently!") provide a model of perspective taking that is critical for handling conflict constructively. Leaders who combine these and similar traits illustrate our notion of embracing conflict. They also would most certainly make our list of the greatest conflict competent leaders of all time.

Traits and characteristics are not the only ingredients in embracing conflict. It also requires technique. In their unrivaled work on negotiation and dispute resolution, *Getting to Yes* (1991), Roger Fisher, William Ury, and Bruce Patton identify a number of steps that lead to mutually acceptable agreements. Two of those steps are enormously useful for leaders in their quest to embrace conflict. First, separate the people from the problem. Conflict competent leaders never fixate on the parties in a conflict. By defining and analyzing the problem instead of focusing on the people involved, leaders begin embracing the conflict while protecting relationships. Second, focus on interests, not positions. By getting to the level of what the conflict partners really want, leaders discover what is behind positions. Such insight and analysis enable continued embracing of the conflict. Leaders who practice separating people from the problem and focusing on interests rather than positions become highly engaged in the substance of the conflict. They become committed to resolving the conflict and confident that the situation can be resolved and that it can provide a basis for continued dialogue, options, and creativity. By engaging conflict with this sense of commitment and confidence, leaders, whether directly involved or playing a third-party role, can establish a tone of optimism that can permeate even the most intense situations.

Philosophically, embracing conflict seems like a great concept. Who would not want to embrace potentially ground-breaking discussions or opportunities to resolve frustrating issues? Practically, though, who in their right mind wants to embrace situations that may appear as ugly, loud, angry, and polarizing as the weigh-in for the heavyweight boxing championship? We do not mean to imply that this is easy. We do mean to imply, however, that those who embrace conflicts as opportunities have a much better chance of (1) persevering through the tough, emotional challenges associated with difficult conflicts, (2) getting to the root of the conflict in ways that enable resolution, (3) empowering the conflict partners to have discussions about the conflict that are safe, fair, and civil, and (4) finding resolutions that meet or exceed the expectations of those involved in the conflict.

Leaders influence conflict effectively in these ways:

- Staying calm
- Encouraging civility, fairness, and safety
- Teaching and coaching
- Providing learning opportunities
- Embracing constructive conflict

Leaders who in the face of conflict choose to act in this manner have the best chances of handling conflict in ways that result in acceptable options and satisfying agreements. Conflict competent leaders are adept at modeling and encouraging positive responses to conflict. As we continue to examine how conflict competent leaders accomplish this, we next focus specifically on their behaviors: what conflict competent leaders do and say before, during, and after conflict.

Constructive Behaviors

The notion of constructive conflict has become more widely accepted and understood in the light of the work of many researchers, social scientists, human behavioral specialists, and adult learning experts. For many of us, the term *conflict* still conjures up negative thoughts of pain, anger, difficulty, injustice, opposition, and frustration. What needs to happen for conflict to be constructive? We begin with a summary of some recent findings.

Constructive controversy occurs when a person's ideas or opinions are incompatible with another's, yet the two seek to reach an agreement or resolution (Deutsch and Coleman, 2000). When engaged in constructive controversy, the conflict partners are able to reconceptualize, synthesize, and integrate information in ways that lead to higher achievement and better outcomes. As compared to other generally perceived constructive methods of resolving conflict such as debate or concurrence seeking, constructive controversy was the only circumstance in which better outcomes seemed likely. During debate, defined as times when both parties argue their points and a third party decides which is best, the conflict partners often found themselves more polarized and closed-minded as the debate continued. During concurrence seeking, defined as times when conflict partners use avoidance behaviors and inhibit their discussions to focus only on agreements, quick compromises may be reached. Often, however, the outcome is unsatisfying because not all alternatives have been sufficiently explored. When engaged in constructive controversy, the conflict partners have deliberate discussions about the pros and cons of proposals and focus on new solutions or creative problem solving. They willingly consider the suggestions and views of the other to produce a fuller, clearer understanding of the disagreement. Then they may find it possible to reach a mutually satisfying agreement.

When controversy is managed constructively, the conflict partners use collaborative and conflict management skills (Deutsch and Coleman, 2000)—for example:

- The ability to be critical of ideas, not people
- The ability to separate personal worth issues from criticism of one's ideas
- An uncompromising focus on best outcomes, not winning
- Listening to others' ideas
- Efforts to understand all sides of issues

Conflict competent leaders practice these skills and encourage others to do the same. Constructive controversy thrives in the world of a conflict competent leader.

At a behavioral level, what do the skills involve? How can we practice the correct techniques and behaviors in ways that lead to improved effectiveness? What are the best ways to reduce or avoid destructive responses to conflict? Let's again focus on the work of Capobianco, Davis, and Kraus and examine seven constructive behaviors that leaders can use to demonstrate competence during conflict. As the discussion of Destructive Behaviors revealed, there are both active and passive varieties of behavior. Similarly, there are active and passive types of Constructive Behavior. The most noticeable and probably the most significant when it comes to addressing conflict are the active behaviors. We'll look at four specific Active Constructive Behaviors here and focus on the Passive Constructive Behaviors later in the chapter.

Active Constructive Behaviors

Active Constructive Behaviors are those in which the individual responds to conflict by taking overt action that results in the reduction of the conflict or the tensions caused by it. These actions require effort and almost always deescalate the conflict. Using Active Constructive Behaviors involves doing or saying things that improve the conflict situation. The four Active Constructive Behaviors are typically among the most useful, effective responses one can choose for handling conflict. As we'll demonstrate and discuss in this section, conflict competent leaders who employ these behaviors effectively realize desirable outcomes and resolutions even in the most unattractive conflict situations.

Perspective Taking.   Perspective Taking may be the most powerful behavior a leader can use to move conflict toward constructive, satisfying, and mutually agreeable outcomes. There are two critical aspects in Perspective Taking. First, there is Perspective Taking regarding content. This requires placing yourself in the other person's position and seeing the conflict from that person's viewpoint. A common reference to this practice is "getting into the other person's shoes." Second, there is Perspective Taking regarding emotion, often referred to as empathy. This refers to the ability to accurately understand and describe how the other person feels about his or her viewpoint and the conflict. It requires much energy and can be hard work, plus it often takes more time than anticipated. Finally, it can be frustrating because the only judge of whether Perspective Taking is working is the person with whom one is in conflict. If it is this hard, time-consuming, and frustrating, why bother? We believe that the results of effective Perspective Taking lead to better outcomes of the conflict, improved relationships with conflict partners, and increased optimism for resolving conflicts in the future.

Earlier we met Jim and Dennis who had a miscommunication about the time of an important meeting. Jim had invited Dennis to a special meeting to make an important presentation. When Dennis didn't show up on time, Jim was quite perturbed. Luckily, Jim was able to locate Dennis before the meeting ended, and Dennis successfully made the presentation. Each had interpreted the information about the meeting in different ways leading to a Misunderstanding with potentially damaging results. We saw how Jim and Dennis were able to turn an unfortunate incident into a learning opportunity. Now let's revisit how their conversation may have been even more constructive with an added emphasis on Perspective Taking:

Jim: Dennis, I was very upset when you didn't show up at the meeting on time. Actually, I was pretty much beside myself.

Dennis: I'll bet you were. I know how important this meeting was. I'm glad you found me, and we were able to recover, even though I had to wing my presentation.

Jim: Yeah, it was better than your missing the entire meeting, that's for sure. I want to figure out why we weren't on top of this, though. How did this happen?

Dennis: I'm sorry for the inconvenience and for putting you on the spot. You know I'd never do that on purpose. I think I just assumed the meeting was at our regularly scheduled time next month.

Jim: When I described the meeting to you, you thought I was talking about our regularly scheduled staff meeting?

Dennis: Yes, I did. I knew it was scheduled for Tuesday, March 11, and it just made sense to me that the presentation would be for that meeting.

Jim: So because we have a standard schedule for our staff meetings, it was easy for you to believe that my request for you to do the presentation was set for the meeting next month.

Dennis: Not only that, but I really didn't think that you'd ask me to do a presentation on just a single day's notice. You're always very good at giving people as much lead time as possible for special requests like this.

Jim: I hadn't thought about that. You're right. I don't like surprises. And I do my best not to surprise you or anyone else on the team. My asking you to do the presentation like this, out of the blue, was a little out of character.

Dennis: Yeah, well, it's not that big a deal.

Jim: Maybe not this time, the way it turned out. And I still can't believe I wasn't any clearer when I sent you the e-mail.

Dennis: I looked back at my old e-mails, and I promise, your message didn't say February.

Jim: Oh, I know. I went back and looked at my sent mail. I wasn't

clear. But it really helps me understand that our communication breakdown wasn't just a matter of when the meeting was
to take place. It was also related to the way I usually make requests well ahead of time. By operating out of the norm, I can
see how easy it was for you to think I wanted you to make the
presentation at next month's meeting.

Dennis: I have to say I really do appreciate the fair warning you always give us about things. I think I don't like surprises almost
as much as you.

Jim: Agreed. I'm glad we talked about this. Now that I understand
how my request was out of the ordinary, it's much easier to see
how I caused you to focus on the wrong date. I'll have to be
more careful when making special requests in the future. It's a
good lesson for me.

Dennis: I'm glad it all worked out. I'll try to be more careful about
making assumptions in the future. Thanks for taking the time
to talk about this, Jim.

Jim: Thank you, Dennis. I'm glad I understand how this looked
from your point of view. I'll do better next time I have a last-
minute request.

The first element of effective Perspective Taking is understanding the content of how a situation looks from the other's point of
view. In this case, Jim took plenty of time to ask questions about the
misunderstanding. He started by asking an open-ended question:
"How did this happen?" This enabled Dennis to provide his view of
the situation. It also demonstrated Jim's openness to hearing Dennis's point of view. Later, Jim used a closed-ended question to check
for understanding: "You thought I was talking about our regularly
scheduled staff meeting?" This technique enabled Jim to test his
perception of what Dennis understood in a way that showed he was
listening. Checking for understanding in this manner is a wonderful way to demonstrate Perspective Taking. Finally, Jim was able to
discern that it wasn't just what was said or not said that led to the
misunderstanding. By engaging Dennis in a dialogue about what

happened, Jim found that his last-minute request was so out of the ordinary that it caused Dennis to believe that the meeting must have been for the following month, not the following day. Without Jim's deliberate attempts to perspective-take, this bit of information would likely have gone undiscovered. Not only did this add to Jim's understanding of Dennis's perspective, it demonstrated to Dennis that Jim was truly open to hearing his complete view of how the misunderstanding occurred. Because Jim so effectively practiced Perspective Taking regarding the content of the conflict, Dennis now trusts more than ever in Jim's ability to consider all points of view when conflicts arise.

The second element of effective Perspective Taking is the ability to convey empathy toward one's conflict partner. Considering how emotional conflicts can be, this behavior is critically necessary yet undeniably challenging. It requires the leader not only to get "into the shoes" of the other person, but more accurately, get "into the heart and soul" of the other person. And at times, it requires the ability to put the need for acknowledgment of one's own emotions on hold. We suggest that for empathy to be most effective, the feeling must be both understood and accurately labeled. The accuracy, of course, is judged by the person who owns the feelings. During a conflict, this can be tricky business.

I (Tim) worked for about a year in midtown Manhattan. At the time, my children were quite young—two and four years old. We lived between Princeton and Trenton, New Jersey. Every morning I rose before 5:00 A.M. and walked to the nearest bus stop to catch bus number one, which took me to bus number two, which took me to the train station in Trenton. From there, I boarded a train to the city and headed to my job as a consultant with a training and development firm. My wife, Mac, rose at the same time as I did, got herself ready for work, and then got Lindsay and Kyle ready for nursery school. While I relaxed and read the paper on the train, she was making breakfast, dressing children, racing the clock, and fighting traffic, all before getting to her job. After a long day at work, Mac picked up the children, headed home, did some chores, started dinner, and then loaded the kids back in the car to meet me at the train station so I wouldn't have to catch buses home.

At the end of one particularly trying day for both of us, I disembarked at Trenton Station and began walking through the parking lot looking for our car. I believe it was raining. It was dark and dreary, and I was exhausted. I spotted our compact station wagon and trudged toward it in anticipation of a warm welcome by my family. I noticed the sounds of rock music coming from inside the car as I approached. Then I saw Lindsay and Kyle jumping up and down on the rear seat to the beat of the music. Lindsay was holding her My First Sony tape player in one hand and Kyle's hair in the other. She was loudly counting repetitions of jumping jacks while Kyle was shouting and playing with a toy dumbbell. My children were gloriously involved in an aerobic workout to the beat of a rock song with a throbbing bass in the back seat of our car! I opened the door to the delighted squeals of my kids and tossed in my briefcase. I glanced to the front seat and noticed Mac sitting behind the steering wheel with her head resting on the driver's side window. I crawled into the front passenger seat, mustered a smile, and said, "Hello, honey." Mac looked at me with weary eyes and said, "Hi, dear. What a day I've had."

Now this is one of those defining moments in the lives of husbands and wives. For the record, this was not a conflict situation (yet). We were just two tired souls longing for the comfort of some peace and quiet at the end of a long day. Mac had just indicated that she had had a trying day ("What a day I've had"). In my consulting job, I conducted training classes in which we focused on interpersonal skills. One of the many interpersonal skills addressed was empathy. I was an expert, or so I thought. And at this defining moment, I responded, with all good intentions, "I know exactly how you feel, honey."

Without getting into specifics, suffice it to say that my response missed the mark of empathy by, oh say, thirty or forty light-years. How could I have possibly known exactly how Mac felt? I had been in New York City all day and then sitting peacefully on the train on the way home. Meanwhile, her day included deadline issues at her job in Princeton, managing children on sugar highs from cake and ice cream at a school birthday party, dodging idiot drivers encountered on the way to the train station, spending an extra twenty minutes waiting for my late train, and enduring a pounding headache as our children "worked out" to the sounds of rock music in the back seat. "I know exactly how you feel, honey" was not exactly what she needed to hear, and it most certainly didn't convey any sense of empathy, even though in my mind, I really meant well.

An empathetic response with a bit of Perspective Taking in this situation might have been something like, "Gee, honey, it sounds as if you've had an incredibly tough day. Want to tell me about it?" The key factor is labeling the suspected feeling—in this case, "tough." For all I know, "tough" might not have been descriptive enough for Mac's situation. She may have said, "Tough doesn't begin to describe the day I've had. I'm wasted." Even so, I would have been in the right ballpark. The distance between *tough* and *wasted* is reasonable, and more important, I would have communicated that I understood what she might be feeling. My statement that "I know exactly how you feel" communicated only that I was completely out of touch with her and interested more in comparing how I felt to how she felt. It was not a smart move and absolutely not an example of empathy!

The essence of Perspective Taking is demonstrating understanding. In conflict, conveying an understanding of another's point of view or feelings begins to loosen the jam of opposing positions. It shows a respect for the other's comprehension of a situation or response to it. When we are asked to work with those who are in conflict, we coach them to focus on Perspective Taking to the satisfaction of their opponent. In other words, the goal of Perspective Taking becomes the conveyance of the conflict partner's position or emotions so well that the parties are convinced that there is a shared understanding. When this occurs, the chance that the conflict can result in a constructive outcome, though not assured, is extraordinarily improved.

Effective Perspective Taking contains both the ability to accurately understand the content of another person's view and the ability to accurately understand the emotions connected with that view. Done well, Perspective Taking communicates these understandings clearly to the conflict partner. Perspective Taking paves the way for cooperation rather than Polarization. It demonstrates a desire to really hear and comprehend the other person's ideas, positions, views, and feelings. When in conflict, knowing that one's conflict partner wishes to fully understand the other can literally transform the nature of the interaction. It's disarming. It turns debate and Disagreement into a search for understanding. It enables those in Discord to pause and consider the possibility of resolution. It creates the potential for even those polarized or entrenched in conflict to find ways to comprehend their differences. It sets the stage for solutions and outcomes that may not have been thought possible. Perspective Taking is not a panacea for conflict. It is, though, the most powerful behavior associated with conflict competence and a tool all successful leaders must employ.

Perspective Taking encompasses:

- Listening to the conflict partner with the intent of understanding rather than debating
- Summarizing the conflict partner's point of view about the conflict to his or her satisfaction
- Expressing empathy by identifying the conflict partner's emotions and demonstrating understanding

Creating Solutions. One of the single biggest challenges reported to us by managers, especially young managers, is their ability to coach others effectively. Many managers become managers after proving their worth to their organizations in a variety of ways. They are promoted after successful mastery of technical or specialized functions. They are asked to take over as a team leader after being a valuable team member. In other words, their effectiveness as an individual contributor or team member is so great that they are invited to assume a leadership role. A common denominator in many of these cases is their demonstrated ability as a problem solver. Organizations love those who are not only adept at solving problems, but are able to do so quickly and repeatedly. But this same skill, so valuable when addressing conflict, can actually impede the exploration of multiple options that is often necessary to reach the best, mutually agreeable, and complete outcomes desired. When creating solutions successfully, conflict competent leaders not only find workable solutions; they also identify and explore multiple possibilities in ways that enable the selection of the best solutions.

There are many ways to create solutions. Brainstorming to generate new ideas is a tried-and-true method in problem solving. Engaging others in the search for solutions often reaps unforeseen possibilities. Considering historical solutions to similar problems or conflicts can be valuable. However, seeking out innovative or different approaches to conflicts may result in new methods of resolution. The key to creating solutions is *not stopping* after finding a viable solution. Finding the first solution is nothing more than ordinary. It's just doing one's job. Seeking multiple possibilities for solutions is the recipe for success. Once multiple solutions are available, conflict competent leaders consider all the possibilities. They analyze the potential of several solutions for maximizing their satisfaction with an outcome. In short, the more potential solutions that are generated, the more likely it is that an agreement can be reached. Creating Solutions is a critical Constructive Behavior that the most effective conflict competent leaders practice.

Earlier, we described a long-term conflict between JT and Vincent. JT was the team leader of a marketing group. He was an "old school" leader who demanded loyalty, hard work, and utmost regard for the good of the team. Flash and self-promotion were deadly sins in JT's book, even though he was in the marketing business. Vincent, a relatively new team member, was regarded by some as a creative genius. He often came up with ideas and suggestions when even the most experienced members of the team were stuck. He loved creative thinking and reveled in the appreciation heaped on him for his innovative style and ideas. But Vincent withered from any sign of criticism or confrontation. Whenever JT even mentioned an issue with his work or ideas, Vincent immediately shrank from view. Over time, Vincent simmered in frustration as JT's methods sapped his creativity and his energy. Finally, at the urging of his friends, he met privately with JT. Soon after, other members of management got involved, and a resolution was found. One member of management, Fay, was especially instrumental in helping JT and Vincent create solutions that ultimately led to a lasting resolution. During one of their three-way meetings, the conversation went like this:

> *Fay:* We've spent quite a bit of time exploring how you both perceive the situation that's emerged. I think you both have a better appreciation of how the other sees the conflict. That's a great step. Now I'd like to see if we can spend some time identifying ways we can resolve the current problem and prevent it from reoccurring. What do you say?
>
> *JT:* Fine with me.
>
> *Vincent:* Okay with me, too.
>
> *Fay:* Let's start by throwing out some ideas that each of you thinks can repair the problem we're facing. What can you each do differently?
>
> *Vincent:* (after a long pause) Well, I can let JT know when I'm feeling frustrated before it gets so bad. Keeping the frustration bottled up doesn't do either of us any good.
>
> *Fay:* Okay, good. That's a start. What else?
>
> *Vincent:* When I have an idea that's a little out of the norm, it would be nice if JT would at least hear me out. I know that some of my ideas are really crazy and won't work. But I think that others are good ones, and if they never even get considered, we'll never know.
>
> *Fay:* What do you think, JT?
>
> *JT:* I'm not sure.
>
> *Fay:* Not sure about . . . what?

JT: It's just that Vincent seems to have lots of ideas, and I don't know how feasible it is to consider every one he has. I know being creative is his strong suit, but we've got a business to run here. We just can't afford to chase every idea he has. I don't mean to be difficult.

Fay: Vincent, what do you think?

Vincent: I'm not saying we have to discuss every single idea I have.

Fay: Vincent, talk to JT.

Vincent: Right. JT, I'm not saying we have to discuss every crazy idea I have. I just want to know that my ideas are appreciated. And sometimes I think we've missed opportunities because we didn't discuss them.

JT: I know I've frustrated you with my hard-line style. I agree that we need creative approaches in some of our challenging projects. What if I more openly seek you out for those challenging projects that need a dose of innovation?

Vincent: Now you're talking! That would be great.

Fay: Good. Let's not stop there. What else?

JT: I think that we could designate a segment of our staff meeting that would focus only on new ideas. That would maintain focus on our project management needs and create a time in our agenda for new ideas. I'd feel better if we could structure how we pursue new ideas.

Vincent: You want to structure creativity? I don't know if that can work. Creativity just happens.

JT: No, I don't mean structure creativity itself. I mean we structure how and when we address new ideas. I'm concerned that we'll lose focus if we just take a "let's go for it" attitude. I promise that I'll be more open to your ideas. I'd just like to agree on some guidelines to help us make the most of them.

Vincent: Hmmmm. It seems a little inhibiting to me.

Fay: What about it concerns you, Vincent?

Vincent: My ideas are free flowing. I don't know how I can be creative if we're so structured.

Fay: Okay. Maybe we'll need to revisit this idea. For now, can we

hold it as a possibility and keep discussing other potential
solutions?

Vincent: Sure, we can do that. Okay with you, JT?

JT: Yep. I don't want to lose this idea, though.

Fay: I promise we'll come back to it. So far, we've talked about
Vincent not keeping his frustration so bottled up and JT approaching Vincent for ideas for specifically challenging projects. And we need to revisit the idea of creating an agenda
item during meetings to discuss new ideas. Let's keep talking
and see if we can come up with some more potential solutions.

This conversation continued for almost another hour during
which a number of additional ideas were suggested and recorded. Not
all the ideas were mutually agreeable immediately; some needed additional discussion. As the third party, Fay demonstrated a keen ability
to lead JT and Vincent in a discussion focused on creating solutions.
Specifically, she helped JT and Vincent identify numerous potential
solutions by asking questions and encouraging more ideas. She also assured both that ideas they didn't fully agree on would be addressed
later. This kept the process focused on generating ideas rather than de-
ciding on solutions. An effective conflict competent leader never stops
with one or two potential solutions. Finally, Fay summarized the
progress they had made and encouraged more discussion. This let JT
and Vincent know that their ideas were being heard and appreciated while emphasizing the need to identify as many potential solutions as possible. Later in the process, Fay would assist JT and
Vincent in prioritizing and agreeing on the most viable ideas.

Conflict competent leaders are called on not only to mediate in
conflict as demonstrated by Fay, but also to use this skill themselves
when they are in a conflict. Had Fay not been involved, either JT
or Vincent could have stepped into her role during their conflict
discussions. The skill of Creating Solutions requires not only coming up with ideas but showing appreciation for potential solutions
suggested by a conflict partner. This can be a challenging process,
especially in conflicts that are severe.

Creating Solutions has these components:

- Identifying multiple potential solutions with your conflict partners (never stop with just one potential solution)
- Discussing the viability of potential solutions with your conflict partners
- Agreeing on solutions to try

Expressing Emotions. When confronted with conflict, most people feel their emotions rising almost immediately. I (Tim), for instance, almost always feel a momentary sense of surprise followed by anxiety over having to deal with my conflict partner in what might be an unpleasant conversation. After that, my emotions, feelings, and thoughts are guided by the nature of the conflict and the relationship I have with the other person. The notion that expressing these emotions, feelings, and thoughts is constructive might seem a little odd. In fact, for some people, it may seem quite contrary to much of what they have learned or been told about appropriate conflict behavior: *Remain calm. Don't escalate the conflict by showing emotion. Lower your voice. Avoid direct eye contact.* It sounds a little like advice from a park ranger on how to react when confronted by a grizzly bear on a trail.

The truth is that remaining calm and not doing things to escalate the conflict is good advice. Lowering one's voice might be a helpful tactic in some circumstances. And avoiding direct eye contact is, in some cultural contexts, appropriate behavior. But what we advocate in Expressing Emotions is much deeper than the demonstration of a calm, controlled demeanor. It goes to the potential negative consequences of attempting to conceal emotions or misusing emotions by directing them in negative ways toward the conflict partner. An individual who expresses emotions effectively identifies and discloses feelings in a manner that demonstrates trust. When communicating honestly, the individual openly discusses issues, thoughts, and feelings in a manner that conveys understanding and builds a foundation for direct dialogue.

Conflict competent leaders practice Expressing Emotions routinely. They do not wait for a conflict to occur. They engage in direct, honest communication about emotions whenever the emotions arise. This can head off potential conflicts before they heat up. And just as important, leaders encourage and coach others to practice the same. Conflict competent leaders recognize the unparalleled value of honest communication and attention to emotions as the basis for effective working relationships.

In Chapter Four we discussed the problems inherent in Hiding Emotions, one of the eight Destructive Behaviors. Among the issues are the likelihood that concealed emotions will leak out at unexpected or inopportune times, the misinterpretation of poorly concealed emotions, the failure to identify or disclose helpful thoughts or feelings, the missed opportunity to build trust through honest disclosure, and the potential personal health issues and stress associated with the suppression of emotions. Given the problematic potential of Hiding Emotions, we suggest doing exactly the opposite. In this case, communicating honestly and openly via Expressing Emotions is just what the doctor ordered.

Earlier we met Virginia, the straight-shooting COO of a public power company, and Ann, the "cool under fire" vice president of communications and public relations. The company had recently requested a rate increase. During Ann's presentation to the executive staff regarding a press conference and interviews about the request, Virginia grew irritated with Ann's deflection of her questions and apparent avoidance of some issues. Both parties were guilty of hiding emotions during the interchange. Later, the two of them met privately to discuss the situation. In the exchange that follows, see if you can spot the key moments when each party took steps toward effectively Expressing Emotions:

Virginia: Ann, thanks for coming by. I am glad we could meet so
soon after the staff meeting.

Ann: No trouble at all. I always have time for you.

Virginia: You are probably wondering why I wanted to meet with
you. I wanted to talk about your presentation in the staff meet-

ing. Specifically, I wanted to apologize because I know I put you on the spot with all my questions. And, true to form, I want to ask you some more questions about the press conference.

Ann: No need to apologize. I'm put on the spot all the time in my line of work. It was clear, though, that either I wasn't responding well to your questions or that there's something bothering you about the press conference.

Virginia: Yes, there is something bothering me. But it goes beyond your presentation about the press conference.

Ann: This sounds serious. What do you mean?

Virginia: Ann, I know I've got a reputation for being tough and mean and tenacious. And I have never been one to beat around the bush, so let me get right to it. Sometimes I'm not sure you're telling us the whole story when you make your presentations to the executive staff.

Ann: (interrupting) What . . .

Virginia (raising her hand) Please hear me out, okay? You've been in the PR business a long time, and you're very good at what you do. There are times when we need you to put the right spin on issues and events. I believe you're as good as anyone I've ever known for doing that. But there are times, like in staff meetings, when we don't want or need any spin to your information. In fact, I want to hear more than just the facts. I want to know how you feel, what you think, and your opinions. I'm not sure that we always get that. In fact, I'm pretty certain we get "spun" sometimes.

Ann: Can you give me an example?

Virginia: Why do you think I was grilling you so hard in the staff meeting about the press conference? I believe there's something that you haven't told us about it. Am I right?

Ann: What did I do to make you believe that?

Virginia: It's a little hard to explain. I think I've developed a pretty good sense for people in my career. Sometimes I detect some—oh, I don't know—variances in how a person is delivering a message or answering a question. I'm a good observer of demeanor. During the staff meeting, I noticed that you

emphasized the interviews much more than the press conference. And when I started asking questions about the press
conference, you reiterated that it went well but didn't offer
any specifics. I pressed you for more, and I'm pretty sure you
grew annoyed with me. Your tone changed, and you stopped
making eye contact with me. So is there something you
haven't told me?

Ann: You picked up all that during the staff meeting? Wow. Well, I
have to admit, I was feeling annoyed with you. And since
we're being honest and up front here, it's not the first time I've
felt that way during meetings with you. You have a way of asking tough questions that make me feel pressured. I bet I'm not
the only one who feels this way.

Virginia: (smiling) I bet you're right. I'm not ashamed of asking
tough questions. I wish more people would ask them. I assure
you that when I ask the first tough question, it's not personal. I
ask because we need to know. But when I think someone is
giving me the runaround, my questions do get a little more
pointed. And I'm sure they feel pressuring, even intimidating.

Ann: I have to say, you are good at asking the tough questions. But
why do you have to make them so provocative?

Virginia: (pausing) Hmmm. It seems to me that we're both interested in finding out just a little more about each other than
either of us has been willing to give. So I'll admit that I was
irritated at you during the meeting. I thought you weren't
being totally honest about the press conference. I may be
wrong about that. But when I suspect there's more to the story
than is being told, it becomes a huge trust issue for me. In my
position, I need to trust my colleagues completely. When I
can't, or don't, it is a big problem. That irritates me. And I
suppose my irritation is pretty obvious, especially to the object
of my irritation.

Ann: Thanks for saying that, Virginia. Not thanks for being irritated at me; thanks for telling me why. I was pretty sure you
were angry, and I was convinced that you were putting me on
the spot with your questions.

Virginia: And what about you, Ann? What were you feeling or
   thinking? And is there something else you haven't said?

Ann: I was thinking that you were being unfair and too tough.
   (pausing again) And I was wondering how in the world you
   decided to enter into the line of questioning about the press
   conference. The truth is that the report I distributed during
   the press conference seemed to overstate the costs we incurred
   during the hurricane cleanup. I was afraid that it might raise
   some eyebrows among the media. It didn't, and I didn't bring
   it up, so it didn't become an issue. I didn't think it was worth
   mentioning during the staff meeting.

Virginia: So you actually thought about that when you were making your presentation to us?

Ann: Yes, I did. You would have wanted me to bring it up, right?

Virginia: Absolutely. If you had a concern about our cost estimates,
   we needed to know. Why didn't you tell us?

Ann: It just didn't seem like the right time or place. The press conference and interviews went so well. And everyone in the staff
   meeting was feeling so good about it. I didn't want to spoil the
   moment.

The conversation continued for another fifteen minutes. Both
Ann and Virginia found that the disclosures about their thoughts
and feelings were instrumental in forging an improved relationship.
They also agreed to be more up front with one another in future
communications. When Virginia admitted to Ann that she had
been irritated, Ann understood why Virginia's questions felt so personal. Ann also respected the risk Virginia took in admitting her irritation. When Ann admitted that she had concealed her concern
about the costs, Virginia verified that her intuition had been correct. This also enabled Ann to understand the importance of honest, open communication in maintaining trusting relationships.

Were you able to spot the key moments during the conversation
that led to effective expressions of emotion? There were several, to
be sure. One pivotal moment was the risk Virginia took to state,
"Sometimes I'm not sure that you're telling us the whole story . . ."

This could have been misinterpreted as an accusation. Virginia leveraged her reputation as a straight-shooter here to say plainly what she thought. This signaled Virginia's intent to be honest and direct during the discussion. Later Ann took a risk when she disclosed that she had been annoyed with Virginia. This was critical because it was the first time either party clearly described an emotion she felt. Often the identification of an emotion is the most difficult part of these conversations. The third pivotal moment occurred when Virginia described how critical trust is in working relationships. This enabled both parties to understand the importance of communicating honestly about both content and emotions.

Not every conversation will be this successful on the first try. Virginia and Ann experienced several years of peaks and valleys in their relationship until this conversation. Earlier attempts at clearing the air had failed because they had focused only on content issues. It wasn't until Ann and Virginia moved beyond content alone and into the realm of Expressing Emotions that they were able to understand each other and truly make progress in their working relationship.

Finally, remember that the purpose of direct, open communication and Expressing Emotions is to foster improved working relationships, especially in the case of conflict. Leaders do not want to encourage complaining or whining in the workplace. The goal is to express emotions in a manner that is conducive to the work environment. Leaders must encourage professional, specific, clear communication regarding emotions and feelings. For instance, saying, "I am frustrated about this conversation," rather than, "You frustrate me," is much more specific and clear, and it doesn't place blame. The key is expressing thoughts and feelings that are most relevant to the conflict situation and doing so directly, honestly, and carefully.

Expressing Emotions has these components:

- Identifying and disclosing emotions to your conflict partner
- Open discussion about thoughts and feelings and their impact on the situation
- Casting no blame

Reaching Out.   The act of Reaching Out may seem as simple as offering an apology. When you have harmed someone in any way, there is no substitute for a heartfelt, sincere apology. Leaders make mistakes. When those mistakes cause injury, damage, or hardship to others, they apologize quickly, directly, and with conviction. An apology during a conflict can be equally powerful. When a person has hurt his or her conflict partner's feelings, displayed anger, concealed information, withheld emotions, raised his or her voice, retaliated, or otherwise behaved poorly, an apology is most certainly warranted. Reaching Out includes this important, widely accepted practice, but it is much more.

The act of Reaching Out is intended to address the emotional harm caused during conflict, reduce tension between the parties in conflict, and enable the parties to fully engage in the conflict resolution process. Some people may think of Reaching Out as a sign of weakness or defeat. The very notion of apologizing in the workplace may seem foreign in today's highly competitive, results-oriented marketplace. Indeed, leaders who encourage others to reach out or reach out themselves may be viewed by some as soft or weak. We suggest that such perceptions are held primarily by those who practice Winning at All Costs with enthusiasm. On the contrary, Reaching Out may be among the most difficult behaviors to practice effectively. It is not easy to admit our own shortcomings or mistakes. It takes strength and courage to own up to an act that harmed someone. It takes fortitude to cope with emotional distress and empathy to handle the myriad of expressions of such distress (tears, shouting, scornful looks). The conflict competent leader knows that such strength, courage, fortitude, and empathy are necessary for addressing the discomfort that can accompany conflict. Reaching Out is often the mechanism for doing so.

Reaching Out can take many different forms. In some cases, the simple act of listening may be the best way to demonstrate concern. In others, engaging in a discussion about the needs of the person may lead to more active steps. An apology may be appropriate. When delivering an apology, depending on the circumstances, finding ways to make amends may also be necessary. Sometimes we reach out to those in distress. In this case, acknowledging the person's emotions is critical. Demonstrating empathy is often one of the first and most powerful acts associated with Reaching Out. The necessity of Reaching Out is simple: during conflicts, especially high-intensity conflicts, someone must take the first step in changing the direction of the conflict. Reaching Out in its various forms is often the expression of that first step.

We've been working with the business manager of a large manufacturing firm. Gary attended a five-day leadership development class with us that included various assessment instruments and feedback from others in his workplace. In general, and of no surprise to Gary, he is seen as highly competent although not especially open with those with whom he works. He acknowledged that this was a bona-fide area for improvement and identified several specific ways he could begin. One of his peers, Douglas, is the chief designer for his firm's products. Douglas is a brilliant engineer who produces results of the highest quality and routinely solves seemingly impossible problems for clients. He does most of his work in isolation and seldom seeks the advice or perspectives of others. He also manages the design department.

Just a few months before Gary attended the leadership program, he and Douglas had become embroiled in a disagreement about how the design department could best respond to the mounting volume of business. During a meeting, tempers flared. Gary suggested that Douglas was incapable of managing the design department effectively during these booming times. Douglas asserted that the design group deserved all the credit for the recent surge in business and that others in the company had no idea how to engineer designs that work. The meeting ended abruptly and badly.

In the weeks that followed the failed meeting, Gary attempted to engage Douglas in discussions about new projects. Douglas responded only to the work requests and avoided virtually all contact with Gary. Projects were launched and completed, but no progress was made on resolving the conflict. Gary knew that Douglas deserved much of the credit for the success of the firm. He also knew that the continued success of the firm depended on a reasonable level of communication and cooperation. But he also continued to see Douglas as reclusive and unwilling to engage in meaningful dialogue. He grew frustrated with Douglas's unresponsiveness to his efforts and resigned himself to business as usual with little hope of improvement.

As a result of his experience in the leadership program, Gary identified his failing relationship with Douglas as a target for improvement. He decided that his personal lack of openness may have contributed to their issues. As we talked, Gary slowly warmed to the idea that there was more he could do to resolve the conflict and eventually revive the important working relationship with Douglas. The primary tactic he decided to employ was Reaching Out. We discussed how he envisioned Reaching Out to Douglas, what he would say, and how he expected Douglas might respond. Gary felt committed to his plan but not completely confident that it would work. Nearly six weeks passed before we heard from Gary about his progress.

When we finally talked to Gary again, it became apparent that the situation was more challenging than any of us had imagined. Immediately on his return from the leadership program, Gary tried to reach Douglas to set up a meeting. Unfortunately, his phone calls met with voice mail messages that Douglas was not available. Gary left both voice and e-mail messages—more than half a dozen over the next several weeks. In his messages he referenced his disappointment in how their relationship was strained. He offered his unconditional apology to Douglas regarding his behavior during the failed meeting several months earlier and asked for a meeting time to deliver his apology personally. He knew Douglas was at work, although their offices were in different locations. As the time passed, it became painfully obvious to Gary that Douglas was ignoring him. Gary's frustration grew. In his estimation, he had reached out well beyond any reasonable person's concept of fairness. Douglas was clearly not interested in talking. Gary saw no purpose in making continued attempts. He had all but decided to cease his efforts when he recalled a classroom discussion about resolving conflict in extremely difficult circumstances. The point he remembered most was having nothing to lose in Reaching Out to a person with whom conflict is polarized. So he sent another e-mail message to Douglas. To his surprise, he received an e-mail reply before the end of the day. Douglas acknowledged receipt of his messages and said that as far as he was concerned, the issues of the past were behind them. Gary was both surprised and pleased. Having nearly given up on the prospect of ever making progress, this was the proverbial candle in a pitch-dark room. Maybe there was something to the concept of Reaching Out after all.

Within the next week, Douglas and Gary met together with a client. Both the meeting and their interaction seemed to go quite well. Because the meeting involved a client, Gary did not have the opportunity to speak individually with Douglas. Gary thought it was important that they communicate face-to-face to ensure that their difficulties were truly in the past. When Gary approached Douglas after the meeting to agree on a time, Douglas said he was very busy and didn't think a meeting was necessary. Gary, surprised again, didn't push the issue. The two of them had interacted in a productive and useful way for the first time in months. This was a start. It wasn't a storybook ending to a conflict by any stretch of the imagination. Most conflicts don't end that way. But Gary decided to be satisfied with the progress and to proceed carefully with Douglas. He would rather build on the small success they had experienced than put stress on the fragile relationship they had begun to construct.

Reaching Out is far more complex than making a statement of apology. Conflict competent leaders, whether involved directly in conflicts or supporting, mediating, and coaching others in conflict, understand the concept of slow, steady progress when dealing with relationships. As illustrated in the situation with Gary and Douglas, it may take multiple attempts to connect with a conflict partner. Once productive communication ensues, the relationship will likely ebb and flow in ways that require one party or the other to reach out again. In addition, conflict competent leaders recognize that interpersonal conflict creates distance between the conflicted parties. That distance, left unaddressed, will not close. A conflict has no chance at resolution if the conflict partners do not communicate or interact. Active attempts to initiate contact by Reaching Out are among the most powerful tactics to use in resolving conflict.

Finally, here is a word of advice for those who wait for their conflict partner to initiate contact. When you are involved in a conflict with someone and you are certain you are the more damaged or distressed party, consider the value of maintaining that relationship. When you have been hurt or embarrassed by someone and prefer not even to see that person from across the room, think about the price of ending that relationship. When you believe you are "owed" an apology by someone with whom you have had conflict, ponder the potential of working together on future endeavors. If you can see, or even just imagine, that potential, Reaching Out to the conflict partner might be the catalyst that not only helps resolve the current issue but leads to meaningful collaboration and a renewed relationship in the future. The best time to reach out is often when you feel least inclined to do so.

Reaching Out includes these components:

- Making the first move to resume communicating with a conflict partner
- Attempting to repair emotional damage caused during the conflict
- Offering an apology or making amends when warranted

Passive Constructive Behaviors

Passive Constructive Behaviors are those that require very little overt effort. In contrast to Active Constructive Behaviors, these often are characterized by withholding comments or refraining from some action. These behaviors usually result in the reduction of tensions associated with the conflict. In general, Passive Constructive

Behaviors are less noticeable than their active counterparts. However, when practiced wisely, these behaviors can lead to satisfying reductions in the harmful effects of conflict and maximization of opportunities for creative or innovative solutions in trying circumstances.

Reflective Thinking.   Our clients often seek our help and advice for encouraging employees to provide open, honest feedback to one another in the workplace. As we discussed in Chapter Four, for many people, avoiding uncomfortable situations and withholding ideas, information, and feelings seem to come naturally. When these practices permeate the workplace, everyone suffers. The potential for improvements, changes, and innovation may go unrealized when people aren't communicating fully with one another.

A common process we use in encouraging more open, honest feedback during our interventions is to engage participants in highly interactive activities and then discuss their effectiveness in working together. Part of the discussion focuses on facilitating peer feedback, a process in which members of the group have the opportunity to give and receive feedback related to interactions during the activities. One of our favorite methods of facilitating the peer feedback uses a list of descriptive adjectives. We ask each participant to write the name of each group member on a note card. Then they review the list of adjectives for each colleague and list adjectives that best describe that person on the note cards. Typically we ask for two categories: what adjectives describe each participant when he or she was at his or her best during the exercise and what adjectives describe each participant when not at his or her best during the exercise. We find that this method enables participants to examine what they have perceived about others in a logical, reflective way. They focus not only on their own perceptions, but consider how they will deliver their feedback in open, honest, and helpful ways.

This peer feedback exercise demonstrates the essence of Reflective Thinking effectively. Several key components of Reflective Thinking are practiced. First, we ask participants to *notice their re-*

actions to one another during the activity. Then we invite participants to *reflect on the impact* they had on each other during their interactions. Finally, we provide time for participants to *think about the most appropriate ways to proceed* in delivering feedback to their colleagues.

When handling challenges in the workplace, even the most decisive leaders often take some time to reflect on the entirety of the situation. They know that circumstances sometimes call for swift, assertive action and decisions. They also know that the highest-quality decisions often result from careful analysis and consideration. When dealing with conflict, careful analysis and consideration can lead to more effectiveness at Perspective Taking and Creating Solutions. Conflict competent leaders practice Reflective Thinking when engaged in personal conflicts and when coaching others in conflict.

Earlier we met Teri and Brad, directors in an organization called Best Solutions. Brad had invited a highly prized potential client to a lunch meeting with his boss. He did not invite Teri because he saw it as a very preliminary meeting and didn't want to waste her time. Teri, though, took the noninvitation as a purposeful oversight. In the days after the meeting, her resentment grew so much so that she decided to pay back Brad by leaving him off the distribution list of her recent trip report, a valuable tool in their company for identifying potential business opportunities. Predictably, Brad noticed the oversight. No one else had been left off the standard distribution list, so he knew the omission of his name was intentional. He also noted that Teri had not responded to several e-mails and phone messages he had sent. His competitive nature and irritation led him to conclude that Teri was looking for a conflict.

Luckily, Brad decided not to trust his first conclusion. Instead he pondered the sequence of recent events and reflected on the overall positive relationship he had with Teri. Let's take a trip inside Brad's head and see how Reflective Thinking works.

"Why in the world would Teri intentionally leave me off the distribution list for her report?" Brad wondered. "And why hasn't she returned any of my messages?" Each of these was a curious circumstance on its own, but perhaps they were connected in some way. "But how?" he thought. "What else had happened recently?"

The last time Brad remembered interacting with Teri was during a hallway conversation about a week earlier. The two had chatted with another colleague about a movie they had all seen over the weekend and laughed about how the characters reminded them of the staff from the production department. There was nothing about that interaction that seemed at all out of place. In fact, they seemed to be getting along famously. The next thing he knew, Teri had stopped responding to his messages. In the meantime, his schedule had been fairly routine except for the meeting with the vice president of World Wide Shipping. "Maybe Teri is angry that I didn't invite her to the meeting!" he thought. "What if she had set up the meeting and not invited me? That would make me wonder what's going on and probably get under my skin a little." Now it all began to make some sense. If Teri was unhappy, perhaps even hurt, about not being invited to the meeting, it seemed possible that she would not respond to his messages. And if she were really upset, she may have sent him a message by deleting him from the distribution list. It all seemed a little petty to Brad, but he had to admit that *his* first reaction to being left off the list was to fight back. So what should he do now?

Brad thought the best course of action was to seek Teri out and apologize for not inviting her to the meeting with World Wide Shipping. He would tell her he would have been surprised and probably hurt if the tables had been turned. Then he would ask if they could talk about what had happened and find a way to prevent such misunderstandings in the future.

The next morning, Brad went straight to Teri's office. He offered his apology, and they talked for nearly half an hour. Both regretted that they had allowed themselves to make assumptions about the other. They promised to communicate more openly in the future and not let misunderstandings spiral out of control.

Brad's reflection on the situation enabled him to choose a better course of action than retaliation. He took time to think through the conflict on several different levels. First, he reflected on his most recent interactions with Teri. He remembered the stark change in Teri's demeanor between the hallway conversation and his phone messages. This enabled him to pinpoint the time frame during which the seed of conflict was planted. Second, he thought through the impact of their behaviors on each other. It was evident that Teri was disturbed by something that had happened between them. It was equally evident that Brad was ready to react poorly toward Teri. This analysis resulted in the discovery of the likely original cause of the conflict: not inviting Teri to the lunch meeting with the client. Third, Brad contemplated the best course of action for responding to the conflict. His decision to meet with Teri, offer an apology, and discuss the Misunderstanding led to a satisfying resolution.

For leaders such as Teri and Brad, directors in their organizations, Reflective Thinking is a critical tactic for confronting conflict. Leaders are extraordinarily visible to others. During times of challenge and pressure, their behavior is magnified and scrutinized. When they react without reflection, their behavior may be perceived as more significant than they had intended. When their reactions are less than exemplary, they are providing an example of behavior that demonstrates to others the wrong way to handle conflict. When practicing Reflective Thinking, conflict competent leaders are models of effective conflict behavior. Others in the organization see the importance of resisting first impulses. They see instead the value of taking time to consider the causes, impact, and consequences of conflict and potential avenues toward resolution. In addition, practicing Reflective Thinking positions leaders as credible resources for those experiencing conflict. When needing assistance for conflict challenges, people seek out those who are known for handling conflict effectively.

Reflective Thinking has these components:

- Taking the time to notice and analyze one's own and others' reactions during conflict
- Reviewing the immediate and potential ongoing impact of the conflict

- Thinking through alternatives for effectively responding to the conflict

Delay Responding. What comes to mind when you hear the word *time-out*? If you are a parent of a young child, you may immediately think of the common reprimand used with children. When a child is not minding, behaving too rambunctiously, or otherwise creating a bit of havoc, parents often place the child in a temporary time-out. The time-out is designed to remove the child from the environment that is enabling the poor behavior and provide a few moments for the child to rethink his or her choices. If you are a sports fan, even a casual one, you may think of the time-outs that teams, players, officials, or coaches call during a game. Time-outs are called for a variety of reasons. The most common are these:

- Provide attention to or recovery time for an injured player.
- Refocus the team on a particular play, tactic, or approach.
- Give players a rest.
- Interrupt the flow of the game when the opponent is gaining momentum.
- Review an important play, rule, or event.
- Assess progress and plans at crucial times during the game.

Both of these common uses of time-outs provide good analogies to the concept of time-outs applied to conflict situations. We call the use of conflict related time-outs *Delay Responding*.

The most important facet of Delay Responding is its utility in providing some distance, psychological or physical, from the conflict. As we described earlier, almost everyone experiences the fight-or-flight syndrome as conflict arises. Our emotions kick in at some level regardless of how adept we are at concealing them. When the conflict begins to cause serious emotional reactions or responses, a time-out, or delay in responding, may provide a respite that lets the strife settle down. Sometimes the delay is requested by one of the conflict partners as a way of pausing the communication for just a few moments. Sometimes the delay is longer: the parties end the current interaction but agree to get back together a bit later.

How do you know the time is right to engage in Delay Responding? Let's return to the analogies we previously described as a guide.

We noted that parents place a child in a time-out in part to remove him or her from the environment that is enabling the poor behavior. At sporting events, time-outs are called when a player is injured or winded. During a conflict, it is not uncommon for one of the parties to begin behaving poorly or to feel injured. When one of the partners feels hurt or demeaned by the other, it may be time to Delay Responding. A conflict partner who recognizes that his or her behavior is out of line may wish to Delay Responding to gather his or her thoughts. A leader who is helping others resolve a conflict and observes sustained poor behavior or sees that one or both of the parties are hurting may wish to call a time-out. At any of these times, removing one or both parties temporarily from the conflict environment may be an effective course of action.

We know that coaches often employ the tactic of calling a time-out to interrupt the momentum of the opposing team or to change the flow of the game. Many people describe their most frustrating conflicts as times when "the conflict just seemed to take on a mind of its own." They report that their worst conflicts just "spiraled out of control." These situations are often characterized by sarcasm and insults or shouting and anger. Or they involve repeated blaming of the other party. Or they career into deadly silence. When a conflict reaches any of these points, it's time to change the flow. Delay Responding can provide the impetus for changing the flow.

Finally, a time-out can be called to review a crucial play or rethink a previous decision. For professional football and hockey fans, we have come to know these agonizing moments as "video reviews." Game officials or referees review video of crucial plays to ascertain that the play was legal, a goal was scored, or an infraction was correctly identified. In the workplace, everyone knows that tensions can run high during conflict. When the stakes are at their highest, every move, every behavior, every statement becomes crucial. At these most crucial moments, the tensions may be relieved if the parties agree to delay their communication with each other temporarily. During the delay, the parties can seek relief from the stress of the conflict and calm themselves down. (This part of the analogy works best if the parties also practice Perspective Taking, Creating Solutions, or Reflective Thinking during the delay. Engaging in these other Constructive Behaviors is not, however, part of Delay Responding.)

Reflective Thinking and Delay Responding may have the outward appearance of being the same behavior, but there are key differences between the two. Both are associated with time-outs or temporary removal from the conflict. During Reflective Thinking, the time away from the conflict is spent specifically focusing on the conflict, reviewing what has happened, and determining how best to proceed when reengaged in the communication. During Delay Responding, the time away from the conflict is spent specifically not focusing on the conflict but calming down by virtue of disengaging from the tension and stress. It is a behavior practiced for the sole intent of allowing the tension and stress of a conflict to dissipate.

Finally, it is critical to understand how overreliance on Delay Responding may lead to the perception of others that one is Avoiding, a Destructive Behavior. In reality, the practice of Delay Responding occurs only during conflicts; someone who is practicing Avoiding never actually engages in the conflict long enough to try Delay Responding. Most avoiders live in fear. They fear that they will lose face, lose their temper, lose the argument, or damage their reputation if they become engaged in a conflict, so they decide not to get into the conflict in the first place. They refuse to engage. A person who practices Delay Responding on a chronic basis may indeed exhibit some of the same characteristics of an Avoider. Our advice is to use Delay Responding as a tactic judiciously. When it is used to calm tension, change the damaging momentum of a conflict, or disengage temporarily from a highly stressful conflict, those practicing Delay Responding will be seen as effective. As with the

Constructive Behaviors described earlier, conflict competent leaders not only use Delay Responding when engaged in conflict themselves, they encourage others to do so when dealing with conflicts in the workplace.

Delay Responding has these components:

- Calling a time-out when one or both parties feel injured or demeaned
- Suggesting a temporary disengagement from the conflict conversation to interrupt the flow of a downward-spiraling conflict
- Creating a pause during the conflict when tensions are so high that the interaction becomes ineffective

Adapting.   How many times in our lives have we heard that ultimate happiness, success, or fulfillment is all about attitude? Who hasn't been reminded that the basic difference between an optimist and a pessimist is attitude? When was the last time you decided that you needed an attitude adjustment regarding some person or event? The final Constructive Behavior we describe, Adapting, is in many ways associated with attitude. In this case, it's specifically associated with a person's attitude and outlook regarding conflict.

As a case in point, let's revisit the conflict between Kathleen and Pat. You'll recall that Kathleen recently made her first ever presentation to the executive team. Pat, a peer, attended the presentation. During her presentation, he made several gestures and exhibited body language that led Kathleen to believe her presentation was not going well. Later he gave Kathleen some rather demeaning and unsolicited feedback. Among other things, he accused Kathleen of "thinking too much," insinuating that she was not intelligent.

Kathleen was surprised not only at his perspective but that he delivered his message with such a condescending and harsh edge. Kathleen remained angry at Pat for several days after their discussion. During that time, she heard that Pat had told others in the department that her presentation was awful and poorly received. She called Pat once to set up a time to talk, but he had not returned her call. Her anger grew. He had been so unkind to her. She decided to wait for him to make the next move. After a few more days, Kathleen's anger began to concern her. She considered herself a generally optimistic person. Why let this one incident color her outlook so? She began to rethink her position. Since she seldom had reason to interact with Pat, she decided to focus less on what Pat had said and done and concentrate more on her own well-being. Perhaps there might be a time in the future to reengage with Pat. She would watch for a signal from him but would no longer dwell on the issue.

Pat certainly could have handled the situation better. There is no question about that. Kathleen genuinely felt hurt. Pat clearly had been abrasive and rude. Immediately after the incident, Kathleen focused on her negative feelings and her sense of dread about future interactions with Pat. Her ability to adapt in the face of the conflict, though, enabled her to refocus and recover. Her decision to remain upbeat and optimistic about the other parts of her life carried her through a difficult, even unfair, time. Although she held no unrealistic belief that the issue with Pat would be resolved quickly, she did maintain an outlook that included the possibility of reconciliation at some point in the future. She decided, for her own sake, to remain hopeful rather than cynical.

Adapting refers to a mind-set of optimism and flexibility. It includes a willingness to consider new alternatives when circumstances might enable a new beginning to the conflict resolution process. An optimistic mind-set is one that enables a person to view a conflict as a problem to be solved. Conflict competent leaders no doubt encounter conflicts that are disturbing and painful during their careers. Their ability to seize the opportunities that such hardships provide and to learn from these difficulties suggests an attitude of optimism that buffers them from angst and despair. A basic premise of leadership development is that leaders learn from experience. In fact, many leaders report learning most from their experiences with challenging assignments or resulting from personal or professional hardships. Those who have an outlook of optimism before, during, and after conflict may have a decided advantage in at least learning from the situation, if not ultimately reaching a resolution. Those who have a pessimistic outlook are more likely to extend their suffering and learn little from such challenging situations.

Adapting also refers to an outlook of flexibility regarding conflict. For instance, people who are willing to consider many alternatives may have more successful outcomes and resolutions. Those who engage in conflict with a preconceived notion of "the only way I'll work with that person again is when hell freezes over!" set themselves and their conflict partners on a path to no resolution. Conflict competent leaders encourage brainstorming and discussion of multiple alternatives during resolution conversations. They are willing to consider various methods, processes, and tactics for solving the issue. This willingness translates into more opportunities and more potential for resolving conflicts that may seem irreconcilable to others. Flexibility supports optimism, and optimism enables positive approaches to tough conflicts.

Finally, Adapting encompasses an element of awareness or watchfulness regarding the conflict climate. Those who become consumed by the negative consequences of conflict consistently miss cues that may lead to renewed opportunities to resolve the problem. Instead, they mire themselves in the gloom and dismay of their misery, blaming others for their plight. They focus only on their sad story of unfairness and misfortune as they relive the conflict over and over. The alternative is to choose an outlook that acknowledges the inevitability of conflict. In this scenario, conflict is not a circumstance that happens to someone; it is a naturally occurring difference in opinion or perspective. It is a chance to see an issue from another perspective. Even in the most volatile of disagreements and conflicts, the Adapting choice holds out hope that a resolution is possible. Kathleen demonstrated this in the aftermath of her incident with Pat. It is this outlook of hope and optimism that enables conflict competent leaders to stay alert for subtle changes in their relationship with conflict partners that may signal an opportunity for renewed dialogue. By staying aware of the evolving landscape of workplace relationships, Adapting leaders are attuned to the behavior of their conflict partners, changes in the organizational climate, and emerging opportunities that may lead to new attempts at resolution.

In the case of Pat and Kathleen, both parties could have chosen a more Adapting approach. Kathleen did. Despite her annoyance with Pat, she chose to maintain optimism and watch for small cues, such as eye contact, to provide her with an opportunity to reengage with him. Pat has not chosen to adapt. As a self-appointed coach for Kathleen, Pat considers his greater degree of experience in making presentations a significant factor in his "right" to provide feedback to Kathleen. From his perspective, he's providing valuable insights to her. He is virtually unable to see any reason to adapt. An Adapting approach from Pat might begin with an acknowledgment of Kathleen's effort. This would send a signal of contrition that Kathleen may notice. An optimist, an adapter, believes such events are possible. This is the subtle nature of an Adapting approach to conflict. Conflict competent leaders stay vigilant for signals and hopeful for opportunities to resolve their conflicts.

Adapting includes these components:

- An optimistic mind-set that views conflict as inevitable and resolvable
- A willingness for flexibility by entertaining alternatives for resolution
- Being alert for changes that may signal new opportunities for engaging in resolution dialogue

Summary

Personal conflict competency is achieved by demonstrating the consistent ability to behave constructively when faced with conflict. We have suggested seven distinct sets of behavior that enable leaders to handle conflict constructively. Every conflict is different. That is why conflict competent leaders cannot, and do not, follow a script. Their effectiveness comes from an array of behaviors, techniques, analysis, timing, and attitude. If the formula was simple and required just a few steps, we would not write a book about it. Instead we would print six billion laminated cards describing the formula for distribution to every person on earth.

Responding effectively to conflict is hard work. It often requires a healthy dose of humility. It requires perspective for considering the possibility that "my way is *not* the only way." It requires overcoming the urge for fight or flight. It requires tenacity for staying engaged in dialogue even when frustrated. It requires vulnerability when revealing emotions or offering an apology. It requires creativity for identifying and considering options. It requires restraint for initiating a pause in the conversation when tensions are high. It requires thoughtfulness when contemplating new possibilities. And finally, it requires optimism that solutions can, and will, be found.

No one can be perfectly conflict competent 100 percent of the time. But we all can strive to be consistently effective by practicing the behaviors we have described. When leaders embrace conflict as an opportunity to expand their vision rather than reacting to it as a source of negativity and frustration, they give themselves and their conflict partners a chance to discover satisfying, even invigorating options and solutions. It all begins with the choices leaders make when conflict occurs. Choose wisely, and conflict evolves into opportunity.

6

BUILDING CONFLICT
COMPETENT ORGANIZATIONS

> The aim of argument and of discussion, should not
> be victory, but progress.
>
> —*Joseph Joubert*

Building personal conflict competence is an important step for a leader, but it is not the only one. In order to enjoy the full benefits that come from handling conflict effectively, leaders also champion the development of conflict competence throughout their organizations. In this chapter, we review the changes that leaders must make to ensure that their organization becomes conflict competent. Some of the changes deal with structures and processes. Others require the proper alignment of corporate culture and incentives to support the types of behavioral changes needed for success.

Benefits of Organizational
Conflict Competence

In Chapter One, we discussed some of the costs associated with poorly managed conflict: wasted management time, absenteeism, retention problems, and time and money spent on grievances and lawsuits. Beyond these out-of-pocket costs, we also looked at reduced productivity, poorer decision quality, lower morale, and

We thank Jennifer Lynch of People Development Global for her suggestions and materials about integrated conflict management systems and Cinnie Noble of CINERGY Conflict Coaching for her thoughts and examples regarding conflict coaching and mentoring.

workplace violence. While these reasons alone are enough for a leader to champion conflict competence, there are more. Sometimes an organization will be forced to improve its handling of conflict as a result of new laws or governmental policies. Other times the need to change will come from a crisis: a strike or class action suit by disgruntled employees, unfavorable media attention stemming from harassment or discrimination, or even a single violent incident, for example.

These crises do not magically appear. They are frequently the result of pressures that build because conflict is either ignored or handled poorly. Eventually the pressure reaches an explosive level, and the crisis emerges. Dealing with conflict effectively can help eliminate or at least mitigate some of the costs associated with these crises. It can prevent or lessen the chances of crises that absorb enormous amounts of time, energy, and money.

Conflict competence can ensure that issues are discussed more effectively to enable better decision making. It can also help create a more satisfying work environment where morale and relationship quality improve. This harmonious professional atmosphere can become a competitive advantage in recruitment and retention because most people prefer to work in settings where they can be effective and enjoy positive working relationships. In effect, developing conflict competence becomes part of talent management.

One of the most important long-term benefits is the ability of an organization to align its internal culture for dealing with conflict to the approach it wants to take in resolving conflict with customers and vendors (Lynch, 2001). Consider a company that seeks to resolve problems with its customers so that they believe they have been heard. If that same company ignores employees' right to be heard, the disconnect between its internal culture and its professed external policy will hamper effective implementation of its customer service effort. In such a case, the links among conflict management, organizational culture, and service quality are very close. Therefore, if the values that are used to deal with one another internally are at odds with the way the organization wishes to treat its customers, the probability of long-term organizational effectiveness and success drop precipitously.

Paths to Conflict Competence

If you accept the idea that conflict competence is an important goal, what next? As a starting point you will need to develop a basic understanding of how systems can be used to improve the ways organizations handle conflict. In particular, we will explore the concept of integrated conflict management systems. These can help prevent or lessen destructive conflict in the first place while at the same time provide mechanisms to resolve conflict when it becomes a problem.

Conflict Management Strategies

Research has demonstrated a relationship between the way leaders view conflict and the strategies their organizations use to address it (Lipsky, Seeber, and Fincher, 2003). When leaders have a zero-sum perspective on conflict, their organizations are more likely to adopt an adversarial approach to its resolution. If leaders see conflict as an opportunity for both sides to gain, then their organizations are more likely to adopt approaches that favor collaborative efforts at resolving conflict. Most leaders incorporate some of each perspective and adjust their approach based on the particulars of the conflict in question. In addition to a leader's perspective, other factors, such as government regulation and competitive pressures, can influence an organization's conflict strategy.

As first described by Lynch (personal communication with the authors, Dec. 12, 2005), an organization's conflict management strategy is actually part of its overall risk management strategy. It has been said that conflict represents the largest controllable cost in organizations (Dana, 2005). We believe that conflict competent leaders recognize the strategic importance of effective conflict management and champion their organization's use of constructive conflict responses as part of building a conflict competent organization.

Conflict Management Systems

The first mention of conflict management systems was in the 1980s (Rowe and Baker, 1984). Early approaches to organizational conflict management focused primarily on the use of alternative dispute resolution (ADR) processes to cut the costs associated with litigation and secondarily on conflict and dispute prevention efforts (Ury, Brett, and Goldberg, 1988; Costantino and Merchant, 1996). These considered different approaches of characterizing the nature of the disputes: one type dealing with the interests of the parties, a second addressing their rights, and a third focusing on who had the most power. They advocated expanding the use of the interest-based approach because it lowered costs and improved working relationships.

More recent work has focused on integrated conflict management systems (ICMS), which embrace ADR practices such as mediation and arbitration but go beyond them. An ICMS incorporates features that focus on the "front end" of conflict to prevent inevitable differences from turning into destructive conflicts. An ICMS permits an organizational "shift to a systematic focus on relationship management through the prevention, management, and early resolution of conflict at the lowest possible level" (Lynch, 2005).

Characteristics and Components of an Integrated Conflict Management System

Conflict competent leaders learn enough about an ICMS to enable them to be effective champions for the right kind of system implementation in their organization. We will present the basic elements of an ICMS together with issues that will need to be addressed to bring it to life in your organization. There is not one cookie-cutter approach for an ICMS; rather, there are guiding principles to adapt to each unique organizational setting (Gosline and others, 2000, section 3):

- Provide options for preventing, identifying, and resolving all types of problems, including nonhierarchical disputes between employees and managers, that are available to everyone in the workplace: workers, managers, professionals, groups, teams involved in disputes, and those close by (bystanders) who are affected.

- Foster a culture that welcomes good-faith dissent and encourages resolution of conflict at the lowest level through direct negotiation.

- Provide multiple access points. Employees can readily identify and access a knowledgeable person whom they trust for advice about the conflict management system.

- Provide multiple options for addressing conflict, giving employees the opportunity to choose a problem-solving approach to conflict resolution, to seek determination and enforcement of rights, or to do both.

- Provide necessary systemic support and structures that coordinate access to multiple options and promote competence in dealing with conflict throughout the organization.

It is clear from these guidelines that an ICMS is flexible with multiple access points and multiple options and inclusive in that it is available to all persons. It also depends on strong organizational support to be effective (systemic support and structures). As can be seen in Figure 6.1 an ICMS contains both components to resolve disputes, known as an enhanced dispute resolution structure, and organizationwide processes designed to promote conflict competence, termed organizational support (Lynch, 2005).

Until recently, most organizational focus has been aimed at developing and improving dispute resolution structures, including elements such as mediation, investigation and fact finding, and arbitration. Indeed, part of developing an effective ICMS includes updating or enhancing an organization's dispute resolution structure.

Figure 6.1. Components of an Integrated Conflict Management System

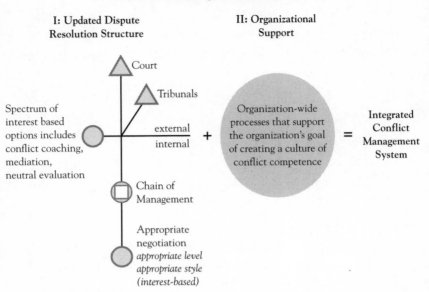

Source: Courtesy of Jennifer Lynch, PDG People Development Global Inc.

This will include ensuring multiple options for resolving disputes as well as multiple access points for entering the system. The structure also necessitates incorporating safeguards such as confidentiality, impartiality, and timeliness, which encourage people to use the system. This prevents people from giving up because they know they will be heard and they need not worry that someone will retaliate against them or think them disloyal.

While an ICMS includes dispute resolution, it also goes far beyond. Conflict management systems expert Jennifer Lynch (personal conversation with C. Runde, Dec. 12, 2005) suggests that 95 percent of the value of an ICMS derives from its organizational support component. When proactive approaches are taken within the organization, fewer disputes will arise. To paraphrase Benjamin Franklin, "An ounce of dispute prevention is worth a pound of dispute resolution." Conflict will never disappear, but it will become easier to manage so that its upsides are realized while its harmful effects are lessened. In the ICMS model Lynch (2005) developed, organizational support includes effective leadership, coordination, internal capacity building and skill development, communication, and evaluation.

Conflict competent leadership requires championing a companywide policy on conflict management. It also means aligning the organization's mission and corporate culture with its conflict management goals, including the commitment of resources to achieve needed changes and the incorporation of desired conflict behaviors into performance criteria and structuring incentives to support the desired conflict culture.

The leader also becomes a model of effective conflict behaviors, which have been described in previous chapters. It is essential for the leader to lead by example if trust in the new system is to be developed. In addition to being a model, the leader can serve as a mentor or coach to other leaders in the organization to help them respond more effectively to conflict.

While the leader may not be personally involved in the details of the coordination, communication, skills building, and evaluation of an ICMS, it pays to understand his or her importance to successful implementation and ensure that these details are being given adequate attention. Coordination starts by making sure that stakeholders participate in the development of the ICMS. While an internal team or external consultants may coordinate the implementation, widespread participation by managers, employees, and others is important because it clarifies concerns, provides a range of recommendations, overcomes potential resistance, and establishes trust. Coordination also includes the recognition that an ICMS is a system with goals that need to be aligned with other organizational policies and practices in order for it to become an integral part of the institution.

Good communication goes hand in hand with coordination. The implementation of an ICMS will face many of the same kinds of resistance that other new ideas usually encounter. Conflict and change are two of the most challenging forces in organizations.

Their appearance together doubles the need for ensuring that a communications plan is put in place to explain the goals of the ICMS as well as the rationale for developing it. There is also an ongoing need for seeking input from and sharing progress reports with stakeholders.

Skill development is another important part of organization support. This involves developing internal capacity to support the recognition and response to conflict early and at the lowest possible level and to help people improve their communication and conflict management skills. While it applies to all members of an organization, it is particularly important for leaders to improve their skills so they can model new standards. Our experience suggests that the use of conflict assessments helps people understand their own areas of strength that they can leverage as well as opportunities for improvement. This enhanced awareness can be coupled with training opportunities for practicing new skills in a safe environment. We have found that the use of simulations in training contexts can be especially helpful in making the jump from cognitive awareness to incorporating behavioral changes that improve conflict effectiveness. Such changes do not happen overnight. Many people need ongoing training, support, or coaching to sustain their improvements and a willingness to engage in new conflict resolution practices.

From a business standpoint, an ICMS needs to be evaluated to see if the goals established for it are being met. The evaluation will identify areas for improvement and provide a cost-benefit analysis of the system.

Creating an ICMS for Your Organization

An effectively planned and implemented ICMS can help organizations resolve problems earlier and at lower cost. The heart of the effort is to foster changes that move conflict from an adversarial process to a more cooperative, problem-solving orientation. The creation of an ICMS typically has a number of phases: assessment, planning and start-up, system design, implementation, and institutionalization (Gosline and others, 2000; Lynch, 2005).

Assessment

The first step in developing an ICMS is assessing your organization's needs and readiness for change. Part of this effort requires discerning how conflict is currently managed to determine what is working well and what is not. It is critical to investigate where and how conflict arises and what types of responses and interventions are currently used to address it. Find out if there are particular areas where conflict is more problematic and determine why this is the case.

In addition, you will need to gain an understanding of how receptive key stakeholders are to the idea of changing the way conflict is managed. Even when conflict is a clear problem, people can still be resistant to change, which can threaten existing roles and power relationships. Part of the assessment process is to build support and secure buy-in for change. This requires affording people a chance to participate and be heard. It is important to share the rationales for pursuing change with stakeholders: cost savings, avoiding crises, improving communication, and improving decision making, among others.

Project Planning and Start-Up

Once the organization is ready, the next step is creating a project management team to oversee the development of the ICMS. With input from key stakeholder groups, this team will help formulate the scope of the program, develop a budget and time lines, and work on creating a plan for the initial design as well as ongoing evaluation and improvement. The project team will ensure ongoing commitment to the plan and alignment with the organizational mission and its policies.

System Design

The project team will recruit others in the organization to help with the design of the system. Some of the most critical feedback will come from people who work in areas where conflict is experienced most directly. In addition to inside help, the project team may use external conflict system design consultants who are familiar with best practices in the field.

After first educating themselves in conflict system design principles, the team should focus on upgrading the organization's existing dispute resolution structure. This may mean improving current alternatives, adding new ones, and creating a method by which everyone in the organization will know what their options are and how to go about making use of them.

Next, the project team will focus on the most important element: building organizational conflict competence by creating support and skill-building structures such as training programs and communication processes. Pilot projects provide an excellent method for testing new programs and can help shape the creation of an evaluation process that includes identification of appropriate performance measures.

An ICMS should be adapted to the needs of each organization; however, certain components are important in all systems to ensure fairness and acceptance. In particular, an ICMS must protect confidentiality and the privacy of the participants and provide guarantees against reprisals for using it. Third-party participants such as mediators and arbitrators should be well trained and impartial. Participation in the system should be voluntary, and it should not undermine legal or contractual rights of the parties (Gosline and others, 2000).

Implementation

When the initial design is complete and pilot testing has been conducted, the system will be ready for implementation. Three key elements comprise the implementation stage: widespread training, continued communication about the program, and increased service delivery from the dispute resolution structure.

Training should be widespread with an initial emphasis on leaders, since they set the tone and serve as models. The training can include many of the elements described in previous chapters: better understanding of the dynamics of conflict, increased self-awareness about individuals' conflict styles and behaviors, and practice using constructive responses to conflict while reducing destructive ones. Special applications related to negotiation and mediation techniques can also prove helpful. Training should not be a one-time event; rather, it should be a progressive, ongoing effort to enhance people's skills. It can be complemented by individual mentoring and conflict coaching to help people put skills into practice during actual conflict situations.

Good communication remains important throughout the implementation phase. In the early stages of plan design, communication serves to explain the rationale for the systems and foster buy-in for it. While these elements remain in the implementation phase, they are joined by the need for explaining the system more completely, sharing success stories (while respecting confidentiality), and informing people how they can use the system to improve their own skills and seek additional help when necessary.

When people have difficulty resolving conflict by themselves, an ICMS provides choices from a variety of alternative dispute resolution processes. In the implementation phase, the project team ensures a sufficient supply of well-trained internal or external practitioners to fulfill the roles of mediator, ombudsman, arbitrator, and other third-party roles required for effective delivery of these services. Once this structure is in place, we recommend using it to address cases that have proven difficult in order to see how well the new system works.

Institutionalization

The final phase in the creation of an ICMS is its growth from a project to being fully incorporated into the fabric of the organization. To foster this evolution, leaders need to make sure that other organizational policies are aligned with the ICMS goals and that performance measures and incentives are used to reward the constructive behaviors that underlie effective conflict management. If the organization ignores the use of constructive behaviors or tolerates those who use destructive behaviors, the disconnect will put the ICMS goals and process in jeopardy.

In addition to maintaining alignment, there must be ongoing monitoring and evaluating of the system to determine if it is meeting its goals. This can involve initial benchmarking of costs and other measures of conflict competence. Coupled with this is the creation of data tracking systems to aid in assessing progress and determining needed course corrections. Ongoing monitoring can also help pick up signs of resistance, which can then be explored. Resistance can often be turned to support by living the model—being curious and seeking to understand the reasons and interests behind the problems people have with the system. This interest-based inquiry, which itself is aligned with the spirit of the ICMS, can enable appropriate adjustment of programs and delivery systems to address all relevant issues.

Leader Roles in Building Organizational Conflict Competence

Leaders have a number of roles to play in engaging their organization in conflict competence. They champion the process and excite and encourage people to move forward in the implementation of an ICMS. Simultaneously they serve as models for the conflict management skills that others in the organization will need to use to realize the benefits of the new system. Finally, they can serve as mentors and coaches to others in the organization to ensure that the entire team models constructive approaches to conflict.

Champion

The first and foremost role of the leader is to champion the process of creating a conflict competent organization. This includes getting buy-in from key stakeholders, ensuring effective coordination and communication about the new system, securing adequate resources and funds to implement the plan and the training required to enhance people's skills, and aligning the organization's mission, culture, performance standards, and incentives with its new conflict management approach.

The president of one of our client organizations recognized that his firm was avoiding conflict at all costs. As a result, most conflict went underground, occasionally flaring up in dysfunctional ways. Finally, the president held a meeting with his senior team to discuss his concerns. The team agreed to work on improving the issue, and training was arranged. The president attended the training and subsequently pushed for the creation of a new set of norms for handling organizational conflict (Capobianco, Davis, and Kraus, 2005). The president's active and visible championing of the process helped make it a success.

Model

Chapters Two through Five focused on the knowledge and skills necessary to develop leaders who are personally competent in dealing with conflict. This conflict competence becomes essential to leaders when they serve as champions. If leaders advocate change but do not model it in their own behaviors, there is little chance that the change efforts will be successful. But when they make efforts to respond to conflict constructively, they become an inspiration to others.

Leaders must show others that it is possible to debate issues vigorously while avoiding personal attacks or defensiveness. They create a safe environment in which there is openness to debate and a sense of shared responsibility. The openness will stimulate cognitive conflict and encourage the creative and improved decision making associated with it. The sense of mutual accountability will help reduce the harmful effects of affective conflict (Amason and Schweiger, 1997). Without the active encouragement of leaders, it will be all too easy for intolerance of differences to stifle debate. Information sharing will decrease, people will become afraid to take risks and challenge ideas, and decision quality will plunge. Leaders need to engage in behaviors like Reaching Out and Perspective Taking as part of the process. If others see them using these constructive types of behaviors, it will make it easier for them to do so as well. This will be particularly true if leaders incorporate these constructive responses as part of their organization's conflict management policy and norms (Capobianco, Davis, and Kraus, 2005; Druskat and Wolff, 2001).

Mentor and Coach

Conflict competent leaders not only serve as models. They also help others directly by providing one-on-one mentoring and coaching to help improve the conflict management skills of others. In their roles as mentors, leaders use their experience to advise and give suggestions to others about how to handle specific conflict situations. Leaders might recommend particular actions to take or specific behaviors to use that they personally have found helpful in similar situations.

The leader's role as conflict coach is distinctly different. Conflict coaching expert Cinnie Noble (e-mail to C. Runde, Dec. 7, 2005) characterizes the skill as one where a leader helps others discover for themselves how to engage in conflict effectively. The leader as coach helps colleagues not by advising but rather by helping them explore or reflect on what they want to accomplish in the conflict and how they can best pursue that end. This is often done by the use of what are known as powerful questions (Noble, e-mail to C. Runde, Dec. 19, 2005). These questions encourage self-discovery, increase insights, and help people reflect on what they want out of the conflict. They also help the individual consider what the other person's interests may be and what options may be available to satisfy both party's needs. Here is an example of the use of powerful questions:

> Fred works in the customer service department. One day he went in to see his manager and said: "I would like to be transferred to an-

other office, where I don't have to listen to Margaret. She speaks so loud and I can't concentrate. I keep telling her to keep her voice down, and she doesn't listen to me."

The manager has many choices here. For instance, she could talk to Margaret directly about the situation; she could facilitate a discussion with Fred and Margaret about the situation or have a mediator do so; she could give Fred some advice about other ways of handling the situation; she could ignore the situation; she could change Margaret's or Fred's office; or she could coach Fred about the situation. At different times and for different reasons, managers may choose any of these techniques to manage conflict. What coaching aims to achieve that other methods are not typically geared to accomplish is empowerment of the coachee to learn how to manage the situation and interrelationship himself. Using powerful questions, the manager may help the staff member figure this situation out on his own.

Consider this dialogue:

Manager: Fred, you sound frustrated. Tell me more about what's going on for you.

Fred: Well, it's not actually all the time, but every day at lunch Margaret calls her mother, who is apparently hard of hearing. She talks to her for a good thirty to forty-five minutes and totally disturbs my lunchtime.

Manager: I'm not sure what you want me to do here. (The manager could then describe the options to Fred.)

Fred: If you could move my office, that would be great, although I guess I'd hear her anywhere with the open space workplace. I have to work with her, and knowing Margaret, she might be angry that I came to you about this. So, yeah maybe, coaching me to manage this would be appreciated. I don't mean to be petty here. I just don't know what to do and thought you may have some ideas.

Manager: I am sure I have some ideas. If you want me to coach you, though, I will do so without suggesting anything just now and see if you are able to come up with something that may work. Fred, what is it about this situation that bothers you most?

Fred: It's her loud voice. She interrupts most of my lunchtime that I like to spend at my desk reading. I don't want to go to a restaurant, the library is too far, and the lunchroom is always full of people talking.

Manager: What is it you need most from Margaret, Fred?

Fred: Respect for my quiet time.

Manager: What is important to you about your quiet time?

Fred: It's important that I get to regenerate. Listening to complaining customers gets to me sometimes, and I like to be off the phone and sitting quietly at lunch. That's all.

Manager: I asked you earlier what you need most from Margaret, and you said, "respect for my quiet time." What do you suppose Margaret seems to need most from you?

Fred: I guess she needs my understanding of her need to talk to her mother.

Manager: And what may be important to her about that need?

Fred: Her father died a few months ago, and Margaret wants to check up on her mother a few times every day. But she doesn't need to spend so long doing so!

Manager: You mentioned that you have told Margaret to keep her voice down and that she doesn't listen to you. What's that about?

Fred: Well, I ask her, and she keeps on talking loudly. She says her mother can only hear when she talks loudly.

Manager: And you told me that Margaret said her mother is hard of hearing. Given that you want to be in the office at the same time Margaret does over your lunch hour, how do you suppose you and Margaret can work out a way to get what you both need?

Fred: She could go somewhere else to make her call.

Manager: What else?

Fred: I've already said the library is far away, and I don't want to have to go to a restaurant or the lunchroom. They're both busy and noisy.

Manager: What else?

Fred: I don't know.

Manager: What might Margaret suggest?

Fred: That I find another place to go for thirty minutes, be-cause she doesn't want to go to a pay phone in a public place.

Manager: Fred, for a minute, put yourself in my shoes as a manager. If you were to make a fair determination of what solutions could work for Fred and Margaret, what might you say?

Fred: Hmm . . . I don't know if you'd say this, but I might tell them to respect one another's wishes for half of the lunch hour. That is, Margaret to be quiet for thirty minutes maximum and Fred to shorten his expectation of quiet time to thirty minutes. Or for both of us to find other places to be. I don't know. It sounds silly when I say this because it's like the classic compromise, and it sounds fair, but I'm sorry Margaret doesn't seem to get my need for quiet and often goes on and on, not paying any attention to my repeated requests. So what would you say?

Manager: I'm not sure right now, but there's a chance that one or both of you may not like what I suggest.

Fred: Maybe I need to talk this out with Margaret. It hasn't worked before, but I'll try again.

Manager: What will you do differently this time in your efforts to talk to Margaret?

Fred: Well, I've just asked her to lower her voice, but I know she hears my frustration. I was a little abrupt the other day.

Manager: What else do you know from your past efforts to dis-cuss this with Margaret that did not work besides express-ing your frustration?

Fred: That she may put me down for being a loner. She's al-ways saying that, and I react to that.

Manager: Putting you down?

Fred: Well, maybe she doesn't mean to, but it does feel like that. Many people joke about me wanting to be left alone at lunch.

Manager: How could you respond in a way that will help this conversation go the way you want?

Fred: I think I might as well tell her that I really need time to regenerate and that's why I sit quietly and read, and I find being a loner at lunch helps me to do my job better. She probably doesn't really know this and just thinks I'm antisocial.

Manager: So where are you at now, Fred?

Fred: I think I'll tell her what's going on with me and ask her to work with me on a way to figure out how we can both use the office space at lunchtime. Maybe we can come up with something. If it doesn't work, I'll be back.

Manager: That's fine. I would like to acknowledge your effort here to manage this situation. I hear that it has caused you some frustration. What did you learn that you will apply in other situations, Fred?

Fred: Mostly that I need to be able to hear myself out—silly or not—and I hope you understand where I'm coming from. I like working with Margaret and don't want to disrupt that relationship. I do have to figure out a way that we both get something rather than risking that we don't get anything.

Manager: Good work, Fred. I'm here if you want to discuss this further, and I'll leave it up to you if you and Margaret want to discuss your options with me, if your one-on-one doesn't work for you [C. Noble, e-mail to C. Runde, Dec. 19, 2005].

Coaching also involves providing encouragement and support for the person's ongoing efforts. Dealing with conflict is not easy, but it can be managed successfully. Coaching and encouragement from a leader can provide just the inspiration needed to sustain an individual's efforts.

Summary

Conflict competent leaders work to make sure their organization engages conflict constructively. This includes championing the development of systems to ensure that people manage conflict more effectively. Creating these systems requires participation from a wide range of stakeholders and may involve the use of external integrated conflict management system design experts. The systems address both dispute prevention and resolution and incorporate training to develop the conflict management skills of managers and employees. These systems cannot be successful without the active support and encouragement of an organization's leaders, specifically leaders who show the way by modeling effective behaviors themselves. The leaders also champion organizational transformation so that a new culture emerges where conflict competence is valued and pursued at all levels. When this happens, constructive responses are reinforced and the opportunities inherent within conflict are realized. At the same time, the pain, alienation, and frustration that come from destructive behaviors are prevented.

Epilogue

Out of all conflict, rebirth and rejuvenation come.
                                        —*Judy Collins*

We began this book by issuing a call to action to leaders: become a more effective leader in your organization by becoming competent with conflict.

We have outlined some of the heavy organizational costs associated with poorly managed conflict. Wasted time, lowered morale, increased turnover, higher absenteeism, grievances, and lawsuits are just some of the outcomes that can stem from mismanaged conflict. We also explored the benefits of constructively managed conflict. Improved communication, open information sharing, vigorous creation of ideas, higher-quality decision making, improved working relationships, and innovative solutions can be expected for those who embrace the potential of effectively managed conflict.

The first step is for leaders to become personally competent in dealing with conflict. Understanding some of the basic dynamics of conflict is an important beginning. Becoming aware of their responses to conflict and the perceptions of others when dealing with conflict is critical for improving self-awareness. With self-awareness comes the leader's need to understand his or her motivations, values, and attitudes that may underlie his or her conflict triggers or hot buttons. Learning how to control emotional responses and choose actions that contribute to resolving conflict round out the leader's personal journey to conflict competence.

Along the way, leaders learn both the language and the behaviors of conflict competence. Constructive Behaviors enable leaders to reach out to their conflict partners, engaging them in dialogue rich with perspective. New solutions are created and explored through honest communication. Emotions are handled with respect and care. An optimistic outlook emerges that underscores the value of constructive conflict. Likewise, Destructive Behaviors are identified and replaced with Constructive Behaviors. Old habits and approaches such as Displaying Anger, Winning at All Costs, Avoiding, and Yielding are reworked, revised, and reconstructed as Perspective Taking, Creating Solutions, Reflective Thinking, and Adapting.

As leaders gain competence personally, the stage is set for encouraging organizational improvement. Leaders become champions, models, and coaches. Champions take the initiative to set organizational wheels of action into motion. They encourage the review of current practices and develop plans for systematic improvements in conflict resolution. Leaders maintain credibility as champions by "walking the talk" as they model constructive approaches to conflict. They support others by coaching and encouraging effective responses to conflict. They also consistently remind all associates of the potential gains when conflict is handled effectively.

Your journey has started. By reading this book, you have taken a step. But it is just a single step on the road to conflict competence. We hope we have provided some incentives for you to continue your journey. Your next steps may include talking with others in your organization about how conflict is addressed or seeking to develop your own skills in specific ways. Personally participating in training programs, taking assessment instruments, working with an executive coach, doing additional reading, and consulting with experts about conflict management systems are all steps to consider.

Your journey will likely be fraught with challenges. It may be long and sometimes wearisome. We assure you, though, that it will be one of the most worthwhile journeys of your life, and we guarantee that you can complete it. The journey requires an extension of the attributes you already have as a leader. Your desire to improve, your courage to change, and your wisdom to choose will guide you. The benefits you reap along the way will encourage you to continue. Remember that conflict competence does not require conflict expertise. You will become a conflict competent leader by understanding a few basic conflict premises, practicing effective conflict behaviors, encouraging others to do the same, and initiating organizational commitment to constructive conflict management.

We believe the personal, business, and organizational rationales for becoming a conflict competent leader are profound and compelling. If you find yourself still on the fence, consider this one final point: the same practices and behaviors that lead to more effective conflict management at work can also improve the way you handle conflict away from work. Engaging in Perspective Taking with your spouse, children, or friends can defuse tension and set the stage for more meaningful relationships. Reaching Out to estranged family members can renew lost connections. A Delayed Response or Reflective Thinking with a grocery store clerk or waiter may preserve everyone's sanity and enjoyment while shopping or dining. By engaging in Constructive Behaviors consistently, you improve your ability to handle conflict anywhere and with anyone.

The sooner you choose to continue your journey, the sooner you'll realize the potential and the rewards of embracing conflict competently. Fights and flights will be replaced with discussion and engagement. You will experience confidence in your new ability to transform differences into innovation, discord into dialogue, and polarization into civility. All in all, your life as a conflict competent leader, and the lives of those around you, will be enhanced forevermore.

Good luck on your journey. We'll see you down the road.

Resources

This book gives an overview of the reasons to become a conflict competent leader as well as the types of knowledge and skills that are needed to do so. Here we list some additional resources you can use to develop your personal conflict competence as well as that of your organization.

Books

We have cited a number of helpful books in the References. Here are some you may wish to read on your own:

Capobianco, S., Davis M., and Kraus, L. *Managing Conflict Dynamics: A Practical Approach*. St. Petersburg, Fla.: Eckerd College Leadership Development Institute, 1999. Provides specific recommendations for improving constructive conflict behaviors and lessening destructive ones.

Dana, D. *Managing Differences*. Prairie Mission, Kans.: Dana Mediation Institute, 2005. Looks at how managers can use simplified mediation techniques to resolve disputes.

Fisher, R., and Shapiro, D. *Beyond Reason*. New York: Viking Press, 2005. Presents practical suggestions for managing your emotions in negotiation and conflict contexts.

Fisher, R., Ury, W., and Patton, B. *Getting to Yes*. (2nd ed.) New York: Penguin, 1991. Classic primer on dealing with conflict using interest-based negotiation techniques.

Mayer, B. *The Dynamics of Conflict Resolution*. San Francisco: Jossey-Bass, 2000. Excellent introduction to the dynamics underlying conflict and its resolution.

Patterson, K., Grenny, J., McMillan, R., and Switzler, A. *Crucial Conversations*. New York: McGraw-Hill, 2002. Best seller that presents a practical method for addressing conflict.

Roberto, M. *Why Great Leaders Don't Take Yes for an Answer*. Philadelphia: Wharton School Publishing, 2005. Presents a powerful rationale for improving decision making by cultivating constructive conflict while avoiding the pitfalls of destructive conflict.

Stone, D., Patton, B., and Heen, S. *Difficult Conversations*. New York: Penguin Books, 1999. Helps clarify the complexity of conflict interactions and how to shift them toward more productive outcomes.

Programs

A large number of conflict management training programs are available. Here are some groups that offer programs we have found to be helpful:

The authors serve as instructors in programs about leadership and conflict management at

Leadership Development Institute at Eckerd College
4200 Fifty-Fourth Avenue South
St. Petersburg, FL 33711
800-753-0444;
www.eckerd.edu/ldi

Other organizations that offer programs which address conflict management and leadership issues include

Center for Creative Leadership
P.O. Box 26300
Greensboro, NC 27438-6300
336-545-2810;
www.ccl.org

CINERGY Conflict Coaching
10 Buller Avenue, #12
Toronto, Ontario,
Canada
416-686-4247;
http://www.cinergycoaching.com

Mediation Training Institute International
5800 Foxridge Drive, Suite 412
Mission, KS 66202-2333
913-432-2888;
http://www.mediationworks.com

Program on Negotiation at Harvard Law School
513 Pound Hall
Cambridge, MA 02138
617-495-1684;
www.pon.harvard.edu

Organizational Conflict Management System Design Resources

For help in developing an integrated conflict management system for your organization, we recommend the following resources:

Association for Conflict Resolution
Organizational Conflict Management Section
1015 Eighteenth Street, NW, #1150
Washington, DC 20036
202-464-9700;
http://www.mediate.com/acrocm

PDG People Development Global
50 O'Connor Street, Suite 300
Ottawa, Ontario, Canada K1P 6L2
613-747-2005;
http://www.pdggroup.com

Pfeffer, J. "Breakthrough Ideas for 2005." *Harvard Business Review*, Feb. 2005, pp. 17–54.

Quick, J., Quick, J., Nelson, D., and Hurrell, J. *Preventive Stress Management in Organizations*. Washington, D.C.: American Psychological Association, 1997.

Roberto, M. *Why Great Leaders Don't Take Yes for an Answer*. Philadelphia: Wharton School Publishing, 2005.

Rowe, M., and Baker, M. "Are You Hearing Enough Employee Concerns?" *Harvard Business Review*, 1984, 62, 127–136.

Runde, C. "Resolving Workplace Conflict: Survey Results." 2003. www.conflict-dynamics.org/cdp/resources/conflict_survey.php.

Runde, C. "Words Used to Describe Conflict." 2006. www.conflictdynamics.org/cdp/download.php.

Stone, D., Patton, B., and Heen, S. *Difficult Conversations*. New York: Penguin Books, 1999.

Thomas, K., and Kilmann, R. *Thomas Kilmann Conflict Mode Instrument*. Mountain View, Calif.: Xicom, 1974.

Thomas, K., and Schmidt, W. "A Survey of Managerial Interests with Respect to Conflict." *Academy of Management Journal*, June 1976, pp. 315–318.

Ting-Toomey, S., and Oetzel, J. *Managing Intercultural Conflict Effectively*. Thousand Oaks, Calif.: Sage, 2001.

Turner, M., and Pratkanis, A. "Mitigating Groupthink by Stimulating Constructive Conflict." In C. De Dreu and E. Van De Vliert (eds.), *Using Conflict in Organizations*. Thousand Oaks, Calif.: Sage, 1997.

Ury, W., Brett, J., and Goldberg, S. *Getting Disputes Resolved*. San Francisco: Jossey-Bass, 1988.

Van Sant, S. *Wired for Conflict: The Role of Personality in Resolving Conflicts*. Gainesville, Fla.: Center for Applications of Psychological Type, 2003.

Watson, C., and Hoffman, R. "Managers as Negotiators." *Leadership Quarterly*, 1996, 7(1), 63–85.

Weiss, J., and Hughes, J. "Want Collaboration? Accept—and Actively Manage—Conflict." *Harvard Business Review*, Mar. 2005, pp. 93–101.

Wiersma, B. *The Big Aha*. Los Altos Hills, Calif.: Ravel Media, 2006.

Wilmot, W., and Hocker, J. *Interpersonal Conflict*. (6th ed.) New York: McGraw-Hill, 2001.

Yandrick, R. "Stress and the Workplace—Conflict Management Can Prevent Behavioral Health Problems." *Behavioral Healthcare Tomorrow*, 1999, 23, 26–27.

The Authors

Craig E. Runde, director of new program development at the Eckerd College Leadership Development Institute (LDI), oversees training and development on the Conflict Dynamics Profile assessment instrument. He is a frequent speaker and commentator on workplace conflict issues and serves as a feedback adjunct for the Center for Creative Leadership. Before joining LDI, he was the director of the International Center for Computer Enhanced Learning at Wake Forest University. He received his B.A. from Harvard University, M.L.L. from the University of Denver, and J.D. from Duke University. He has practiced law in Colorado and has taught at the University of Minnesota Law School and Wake Forest University.

Tim A. Flanagan is director of custom programs at the Leadership Development Institute (LDI) at Eckerd College, St. Petersburg, Florida. He oversees business management and program design for customized leadership and organizational development programming at LDI. In addition, he is a senior instructor for the Center for Creative Leadership programs conducted at LDI, as well as all other open enrollment and custom programs at the institute. He teaches in the Rollins College Executive and Management Education program and the Western Management Development Center. Tim has managed executive development and training programs internally and has consulted with hundreds of organizations in his career. He received his B.A. from Muskingum College, New Concord, Ohio, and M.A. from the Ohio State University, Columbus, Ohio.

Index

About the Center for Creative Leadership

The Center for Creative Leadership (CCL) is a nonprofit, educational institution with international reach. Since the Center's founding in 1970, its mission has been to advance the understanding, practice, and development of leadership for the benefit of society worldwide.

Devoted to leadership education and research, CCL works annually with more than two thousand organizations and twenty thousand individuals from the private, public, education, and nonprofit sectors. The Center's five campuses span three continents: Greensboro, North Carolina; Colorado Springs, Colorado; and San Diego, California, in North America; Brussels, Belgium, in Europe; and Singapore in Asia. In addition, sixteen Network Associates around the world offer selected CCL programs and assessments.

CCL draws strength from its nonprofit status and educational mission, which provide unusual flexibility in a world where quarterly profits often drive thinking and direction. It has the freedom to be objective, wary of short-term trends, and motivated foremost by its mission—hence our substantial and sustained investment in leadership research. Although CCL's work is always grounded in a strong foundation of research, it focuses on achieving a beneficial impact in the real world. Its efforts are geared to be practical and action oriented, helping leaders and their organizations more effectively achieve their goals and vision. The desire to transform learning and ideas into action provides the impetus for CCL's programs, assessments, publications, and services.

Capabilities

CCL's activities encompass leadership education, knowledge generation and dissemination, and building a community centered on leadership. CCL is broadly recognized for excellence in executive education, leadership development, and innovation by sources such as *BusinessWeek*, the *Financial Times*, the *New York Times*, and the *Wall Street Journal*.

Open-Enrollment Programs

Fourteen open-enrollment courses are designed for leaders at all levels, as well as people responsible for leadership development and training at their organizations. This portfolio offers distinct choices for participants seeking a particular learning environment or type of experience. Some programs are structured specifically around small group activities, discussion, and personal reflection, while others offer hands-on opportunities through business simulations, artistic exploration, team-building exercises, and new-skills practice. Many of these programs offer private one-on-one sessions with a feedback coach.

For a complete listing of programs, visit http://www.ccl.org/programs.

Customized Programs

CCL develops tailored educational solutions for more than one hundred client organizations around the world each year. Through this applied practice, CCL structures and delivers programs focused on specific leadership development needs within the context of defined organizational challenges, including innovation, the merging of cultures, and the development of a broader pool of leaders. The objective is to help organizations develop, within their own cultures, the leadership capacity they need to address challenges as they emerge.

Program details are available online at http://www.ccl.org/custom.

Coaching

CCL's suite of coaching services is designed to help leaders maintain a sustained focus and generate increased momentum toward achieving their goals. These coaching alternatives vary in depth and duration and serve a variety of needs, from helping an executive sort through career and life issues to working with an organization to integrate coaching into its internal development process. Our coaching offerings, which can supplement program attendance or be customized for specific individual or team needs, are based on our ACS model of assessment, challenge, and support.

Learn more about CCL's coaching services at http://www.ccl.org/coaching.

Assessment and Development Resources

CCL pioneered 360-degree feedback and believes that assessment provides a solid foundation for learning, growth, and transformation and that development truly happens when an individual recognizes the need to change. CCL offers a broad selection of assessment tools, online resources, and simulations that can help individuals, teams, and organizations increase their self-awareness, facilitate their own learning, enable their development, and enhance their effectiveness.

CCL's assessments are profiled at http://www.ccl.org/assessments.

Publications

The theoretical foundation for many of our programs, as well as the results of CCL's extensive and often groundbreaking research, can be found in the scores of publications issued by CCL Press and through the Center's alliance with Jossey-Bass, a Wiley imprint. Among these are landmark works, such as *Breaking the Glass Ceiling, The*

Lessons of Experience, and *The Center for Creative Leadership Handbook of Leadership Development*, as well as quick-read guidebooks focused on core aspects of leadership. CCL publications provide insights and practical advice to help individuals become more effective leaders, develop leadership training within organizations, address issues of change and diversity, and build the systems and strategies that advance leadership collectively at the institutional level.

A complete listing of CCL publications is available at http://www.ccl.org/publications.

Leadership Community

To ensure that the Center's work remains focused, relevant, and important to the individuals and organizations it serves, CCL maintains a host of networks, councils, and learning and virtual communities that bring together alumni, donors, faculty, practicing leaders, and thought leaders from around the globe. CCL also forges relationships and alliances with individuals, organizations, and associations that share its values and mission. The energy, insights, and support from these relationships help shape and sustain CCL's educational and research practices and provide its clients with an added measure of motivation and inspiration as they continue their lifelong commitment to leadership and learning.

To learn more, visit http://www.ccl.org/connected.

Research

CCL's portfolio of programs, products, and services is built on a solid foundation of behavioral science research. The role of research at CCL is to advance the understanding of leadership and to transform learning into practical tools for participants and clients. CCL's research is the hub of a cycle that transforms knowledge into applications and applications into knowledge, thereby illuminating the way organizations think about and enact leadership and leader development.

Find out more about current research initiatives at http://www.ccl.org/research.

For additional information about CCL, please visit http://www.ccl.org or call Client Services at 336-545-2810.